THE HOW AND WHY WONDER BOOK OF
FLIGHT

Written by HAROLD JOSEPH HIGHLAND, B.S., M.S., Ph.D.
Associate Professor, College of Business Administration,
Long Island University

Illustrated by GEORGE J. ZAFFO

Editorial Production: DONALD D. WOLF

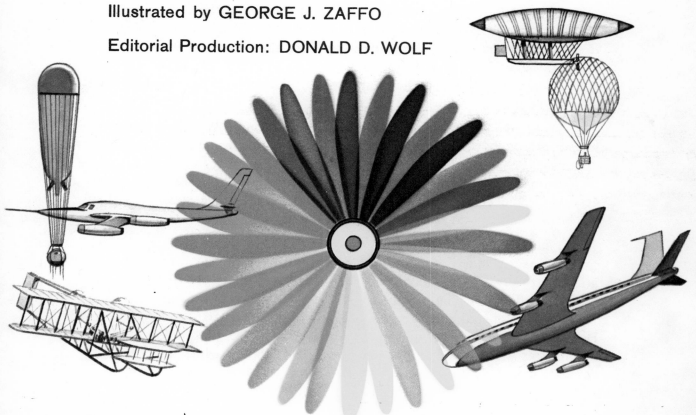

Edited under the supervision of
    Dr. Paul E. Blackwood.
    Washington, D. C.

Text and illustrations approved by
    Oakes A. White, Brooklyn Children's Museum, Brooklyn, New York

GROSSET & DUNLAP • **Publishers** • **NEW YORK**

Introduction

Scientists are filled with curiosity and this leads them to search for answers through exploration and experiment. This *How and Why Wonder Book* amply demonstrates how, over the years, the search for ways to move through the air has led to present-day miracles of flight. The book will help young scientists to widen their horizons of discovery about the unending efforts to conquer and explore space.

To fly like a bird has always been a hope of man. We know this from legend, mythology and recorded history. The hope has burned in man's dreams and challenged him to make the attempt. First it seemed like a dream of improbable fulfillment. Then gradually, from fumbling beginnings, success was achieved. Man flew! And now, in many ways, he flies better than the birds—higher and faster and beyond the air.

The How and Why Wonder Book of Flight helps the reader to relive the fascinating story of man's increasing mastery of the air from early attempts to present-day accomplishments. It takes the reader from the first flight of balloons, which merely drifted with the wind, to the amazing X-15 with its phenomenal speeds and man's orbiting of the earth in a spaceship. Here are answers to many questions about early types of planes, jets, missiles and rockets. Why does an airplane fly? What is the jet stream? How do pilots navigate in bad weather? And many others.

Every person who is excited about living in the space age, at a time when man continues his effort to explore the solar system and when scheduled flights may well carry passengers to the moon, should have this book of basic information about flight for reading and reference.

Paul E. Blackwood

Dr. Blackwood is a professional employee in the U. S. Office of Education. This book was edited by him in his private capacity and no official support or endorsement by the Office of Education is intended or should be inferred.

Contents

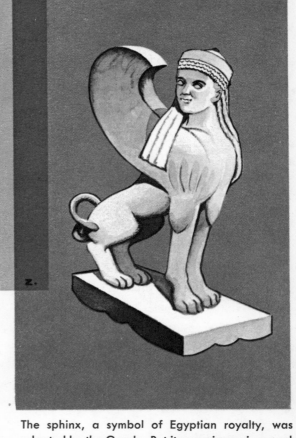

Man gave the power of flight to gods and sacred animals. The winged bull is an Assyrian sculpture of the ninth century B.C.

The sphinx, a symbol of Egyptian royalty, was adopted by the Greeks. But it was given wings and served as tomb sculpture in the sixth century B.C.

This detail from a Greek vase of the fourth century B.C. shows the mythical hero Bellerophon mounted on his winged horse Pegasus. Together, they slew the three-headed Chimera. Sculptures similar to these are exhibited at the Metropolitan Museum of Art, New York.

Dreams of Flight

The story of man's dream of flight, of his desire to reach the stars, is as old as mankind itself. It is easy to imagine that prehistoric man, faced with a fierce, attacking monster, yearned to spring up and fly away just like a bird.

In ancient folklore and religions, we have ample proof of this desire to fly. But desires and dreams cannot lift a man off the earth, and so the wondrous ability to fly was reserved for his gods. Each of the gods had some means of flight. In ancient Greece, Phaeton, son of Helios, the sun god, drove the wild horses that pulled the sun chariot. Mercury, the messenger of the gods, had a winged helmet and winged sandals. The

Out of man's ancient dream of flight came this extension of his desire — a winged lion (Middle Ages).

The woodcut by the German painter and engraver, Albrecht Dürer, depicts Daedalus and Icarus fleeing the island of Crete. But Icarus perished in the sea.

winged horse, Pegasus, was able to fly faster, farther and higher than any bird.

The dream of flight was universal. In ancient Egypt and Babylonia, they pictured winged bulls, winged lions and even men with wings. The ancient Chinese, Greeks, Aztecs of Central America, Iroquois of North America, all shared this dream.

According to Greek legend, Daedalus,

Who was the first man to fly? the Athenian inventor, was the first man to fly. He and his son, Icarus, had been imprisoned on the island of Crete by King Minos. In order to escape, Daedalus shaped wings of wax into which he stuck bird feathers.

During their flight, Icarus flew too high and the sun melted the wax. He was drowned in the sea, and that body of water is still called the Icarian Sea in honor of the first man to lose his life in flying. The father is supposed to have continued his flight and reached Sicily, several hundred miles away.

There is also an English legend of King Bladud who, during his reign in the ninth century B.C., used wings to fly. But his flight was short-lived and he fell to his death.

The dream of flying continued, but in all the legends, the flier rose like a bird only to fall like a stone. It was more than twenty-six hundred years after King Bladud's flight that men flew up into the air and returned to earth safely.

The first man to approach flying on a

What is ethereal air? scientific basis was Roger Bacon, an Englishman who lived during the thirteenth century. He envisioned the air about us as a sea, and he believed that a balloon could float on the air just as a boat did on water. His balloon, or air boat, was to be filled with *ethereal air* so that it might float on the air sea. We do not know what Bacon meant by ethereal air; yet, many still credit him with the basic concept of balloon flight.

Almost four hundred years later, Francesco de Lana, an Italian priest, applied Bacon's principle of air flight. He designed a boat, complete with mast

A Frenchman named Besnier claimed that he flew the above contraption in the late seventeenth century.

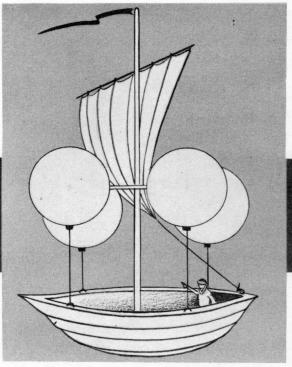

De Lana's air boat was held aloft by four spheres.

6

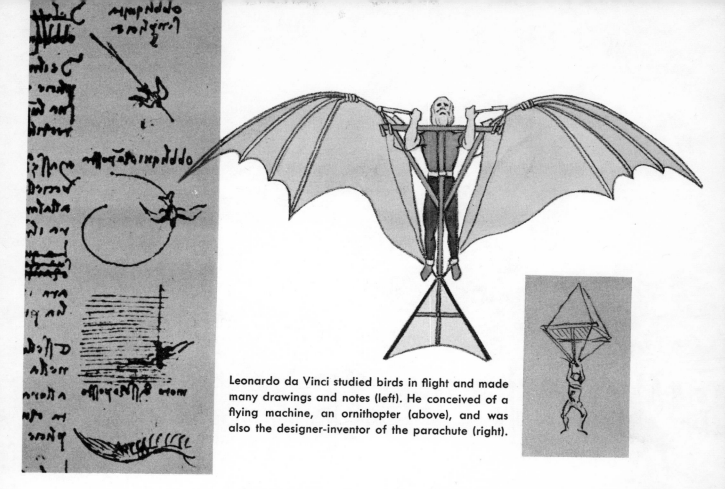

Leonardo da Vinci studied birds in flight and made many drawings and notes (left). He conceived of a flying machine, an ornithopter (above), and was also the designer-inventor of the parachute (right).

and sail, which would be held in the air by four hollow spheres. Each of the four balls was to be 20 feet in diameter and made of very thin copper. The air was to be removed from the balls so that they could float in the sky and lift the boat into the air.

De Lana's boat was never built since it was not possible to make spheres of such thin metal and such size in those days. Even if they had been built, the thin spheres would have been crushed by the pressure of the atmosphere.

Leonardo da Vinci was not only the greatest mathematician of the fifteenth century, but also a noted painter, architect, sculptor, engineer and musician. After studying the flight of birds and the movement of the air,

What is an ornithopter?

he reasoned that birds flew because they flapped their wings and that it was possible for man to do the same. Da Vinci designed the *ornithopter* (or-ni-THOP-ter), a flapping-wing flying machine. The wings were to be moved by a man's arms and legs.

Ornithopters were tried by many men. Robert Hooke experimented with this means of flight in England about 1650. He claimed he succeeded in flying, but he also wrote of his great difficulties to remain in the air. He is the first man who recognized that feathers were not needed for flight.

Many men tried and failed to fly with the ornithopter. It was not until 1890 that Octave Chanute discovered why this method would never succeed — man could not develop sufficient power with only his arms and legs.

The first balloon flights were made in 1783 when the Montgolfier brothers used heated air to make an ornate balloon rise.

One of the memorable early balloon flights was made by J. A. C. Charles, a French physicist, and one of the Robert brothers. The flight lasted over two hours, reaching a two-mile height.

The Age of Aerostatics

How did aerostatics help man to fly?

In 1643, Evangelista Torricelli demonstrated that the earth's atmosphere is more than just empty space. With his barometer, he proved that the atmosphere has weight and density, just like any gas. This discovery was the beginning of the science of *aerostatics*. Aerostatics (aero-STAT-ics) is the study of how an object is supported in the air by buoyancy; that is, its ability to float in air as a boat floats on water.

A milestone in this new science was reached ten years before the Declaration of Independence. Henry Cavendish, an English scientist, mixed iron, tin and zinc shavings with oil of vitriol and discovered a new gas which was lighter than air. Cavendish's "inflammable air" was later named "hydrogen" by the French chemist, Lavoisier.

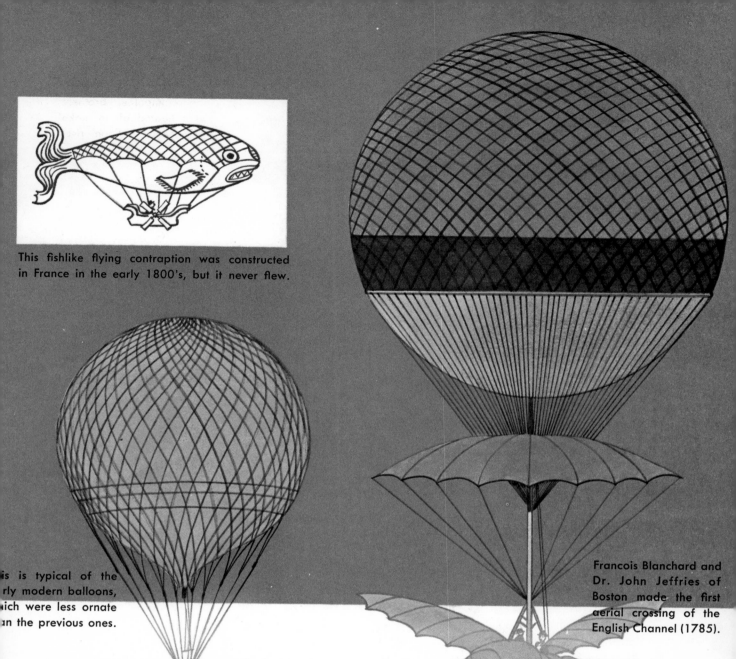

This fishlike flying contraption was constructed in France in the early 1800's, but it never flew.

...is is typical of the ...rly modern balloons, ...ich were less ornate ...an the previous ones.

Francois Blanchard and Dr. John Jeffries of Boston made the first aerial crossing of the English Channel (1785).

Some sixteen years after Cavendish discovered his new gas, Joseph and Jacques Montgolfier, French ornithoptists, were fascinated by watching smoke travel up from the fireplace through the chimney. They conceived the idea of making a smoke cloud which would fly in the air. They took a lightweight bag, filled it with smoke, and watched it float through the air.

How did the first balloonists fly?

After numerous experiments, they made a large linen bag, about 110 feet in circumference. At Annonay, in late 1783, they had the bag suspended over a fire of wool and straw in order to fill it with smoke. The smoke-filled bag rose almost 6,000 feet into the air and stayed afloat for 10 minutes. It fell to earth, as the heated gas inside the bag cooled, landing a couple of miles away. A man-made object had actually flown.

With the French Royal Academy of Sciences, the brothers built a larger balloon, 41 feet in diameter. It carried

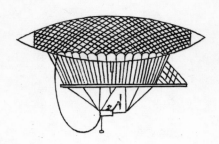

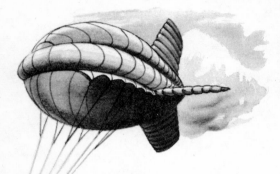

Henri Giffard built the first successful dirigible (top left) in 1852. It was powered by a propeller driven by a steam engine. The first controllable dirigible (above) was built by Alberto Santos-Dumont. Barrage balloons (left) were used in World Wars I and II to prevent low-level flying attacks by enemy planes.

some 400 to 500 pounds into the air, thus proving that it was possible to lift a man. On September 19, 1783, the new balloon carried its first passengers — a duck, a rooster and a sheep, and returned them safely to earth. Less than one month later, the first human ascent was made. Jean Francois Pilâtre de Rozier stayed aloft for over 4 minutes and reached a height of almost 85 feet.

Shortly after Pilâtre de Rozier took the

Why did the hydrogen balloon fly?

first balloon flight, J. A. C. Charles, a French physicist, filled a rubber-coated silk balloon with hydrogen, which Cavendish had discovered. This balloon rose more rapidly than the earlier ones, remained in flight for almost 45 minutes, and landed over 16 miles away. Professor Charles raced after the balloon, but when he arrived he found the peasants using pitchforks to kill the unknown "monster."

The *Charlière,* as hydrogen balloons were called for many years, rose rapidly

because hydrogen is considerably lighter than smoke or air. The weight of the air in a balloon that is about 3½ feet in diameter is 8 pounds. The weight of hydrogen in a similar balloon is only ½ pound.

The greatest of the early balloonists was

Who were other famous early balloonists?

Francois Blanchard, who demonstrated balloon flying all over Europe and made the first American balloon flight on January 9, 1793. His most famous flight was across the English Channel in 1785, when he established the first international air mail on record.

Another famous early balloonist was Captain Coutelle of the French Revolutionary Army, who manned the first

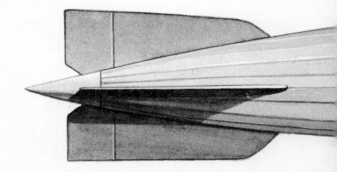

The zeppelin had a metal frame in which "bags" of hydrogen were used to make the craft "float."

balloon used in warfare. In 1794, at the battle of Fleurus, the captain signaled information to General Jourdan, who was able to take advantage of the shifting battle situation and emerged victorious.

The early balloons consisted of an inflated bag to which an open basket, or *gondola* (GON-do-la), was attached by ropes. To

How does a dirigible differ from a balloon?

make the balloon go higher into the air, the "pilot" lightened its weight by dropping bags of sand, which were secured to the sides of the gondola. To make the balloon descend, he opened a valve and let some of the gas escape. The balloon rose into the air, but there was no way to control its flight. Once aloft, the balloon — and the men with it — were at the mercy of the winds.

The *dirigible* (DIR-i-gi-ble), or airship as it is sometimes called, can be steered. It consists of an elongated, gas-filled bag with cars, or gondolas, below for passengers and power. The dirigible takes advantage of the wind, but also uses motor-driven propellers. The early dirigibles used a sliding weight to make them go up or down. Pushing the weight toward the front pointed the nose of the airship down; conversely, with the weight toward the back, the nose pointed upward. Later dirigibles used horizontal tail fins to direct their upward and downward movement. Vertical tail fins were used to steer them right and left.

In 1852, almost seventy years after the first Montgolfier balloon rose over Annonay, a French engineer, Henri Giffard, built the first successful dirigible. Shaped like a cigar, it was 143 feet long and was powered by a 3-horsepower steam engine with a propeller attached to the gondola. Because of its low speed, under 5 miles per hour, this airship was pushed backward in a strong wind.

When did the first dirigible fly?

The first dirigible which could be accurately controlled and guided was *Airship Number One,* built by Alberto Santos-Dumont, a Brazilian millionaire living in France. In 1901, he flew his airship around the Eiffel Tower in Paris.

The early dirigibles were nonrigid; that is, they were long gas-filled bags. A gondola and powered propeller were attached. When longitudinal framing, running the length of the bag, was used as reinforcement, the semi-rigid dirigible was created.

What is a zeppelin?

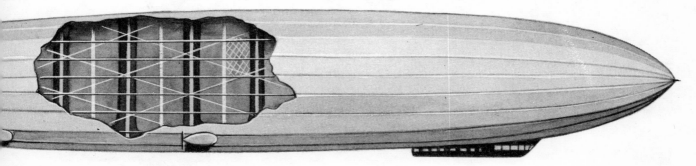

PLANES OF WORLD WAR 1

FOKKER (D-7)

SPAD

SE-5

R. WALFISH (WHALE)

ORNITHOPTER

BALLOON

MERCURY,
THE WINGED GOD

WRIGHT PLANE (1905)

FLYING BOAT (1920)

FORD MONOPLANE (

FOKKER (E-4)

HANDLEY-PAGE BOMBER (400)

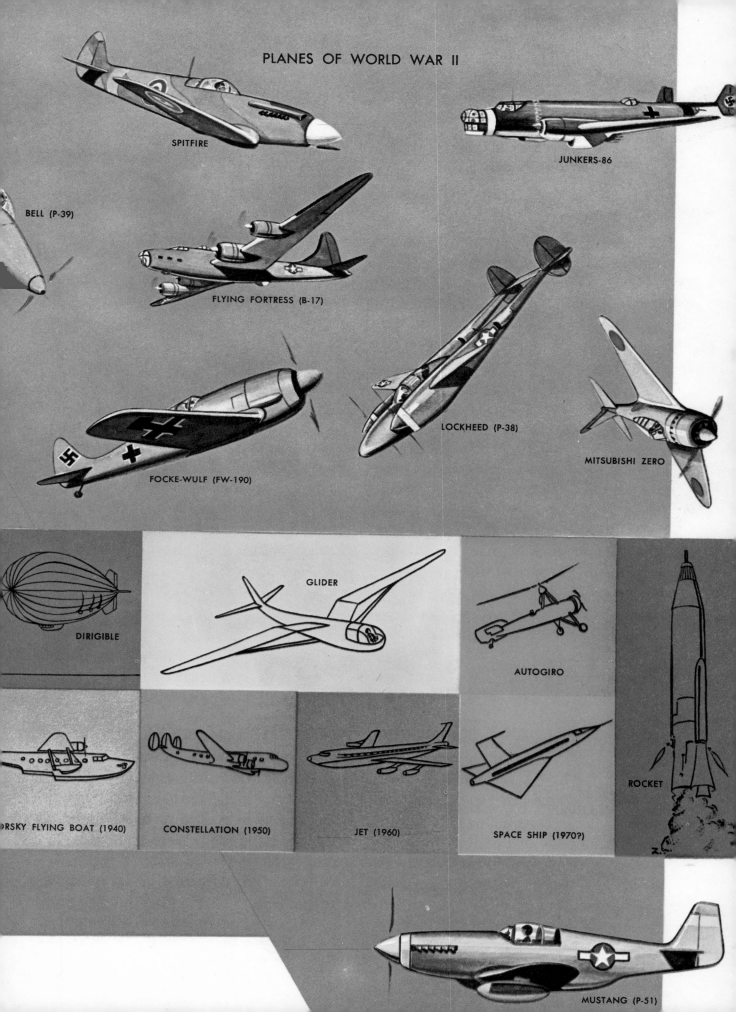

PLANES OF WORLD WAR II

SPITFIRE

JUNKERS-86

BELL (P-39)

FLYING FORTRESS (B-17)

FOCKE-WULF (FW-190)

LOCKHEED (P-38)

MITSUBISHI ZERO

DIRIGIBLE

GLIDER

AUTOGIRO

ROCKET

SIKORSKY FLYING BOAT (1940)

CONSTELLATION (1950)

JET (1960)

SPACE SHIP (1970?)

MUSTANG (P-51)

The rigid dirigible, or *zeppelin* (ZEP-pe-lin), was first built by Count Ferdinand von Zeppelin of Germany in 1899. This type, as contrasted with the non-rigid and semi-rigid, had a complete rigid framework covered with fabric. Inside the frame were several gas-filled balloons, and below the frame was a cabin for the crew. It was 155 feet long and 40 feet in diameter.

During World War I, the Germans used zeppelins to drop bombs from the sky. After the war, other countries, including the United States, began to build zeppelin-type airships. In 1919, the British R-34 made the first transatlantic airship flight between England and the United States.

In 1929, the Graf Zeppelin took about ten days (flying time), traveling almost 22,000 miles, to go completely around the earth. Bigger and faster zeppelins were built, and they carried passengers, freight and mail to many sections of the world. The largest of these was the

Hindenburg which was 830 feet long and 135 feet in diameter.

Two factors contributed to the decline of the zeppelins. First, those filled with hydrogen were very dangerous, since hydrogen explodes and burns. The last hydrogen-filled zeppelin seen outside of Germany was the *Hindenburg,* which exploded and burned in May, 1937, while landing at Lakehurst, New Jersey.

Why did the zeppelin disappear?

Although the United States used *helium* (HE-li-um), a natural gas which does not burn, its airships, the *Akron* and *Macon,* were both lost. They were destroyed by bad weather, the second factor which caused the decline of zeppelin-type airships.

Small, nonrigid airships, or blimps, are still used for offshore anti-submarine patrol duty and to explore the edges of space, but large, rigid airships are part of history.

The Air Pioneers

Sir George Cayley has been called the father of *aeronautics* (aer-o-NAU-tics). This is the science of flight, including the principles and techniques of building and flying balloons, airships and airplanes, as well as *aerodynamics* (aer-o-dy-NAM-ics), the science of air in motion and the movement of bodies through the air.

Who is the father of aeronautics?

This early nineteenth century Englishman denounced ornithopters as impractical. Drawing upon an earlier discovery, Cayley decided that it would be possible to make a plane fly through the air if the plane were light enough, and if air could be forced against its wings by moving the plane through the air.

He solved the problem of making the

14

plane light by using diagonal bracing to reinforce the wings and body instead of using solid pieces of wood. The second problem, moving the ship through the air, was to be solved by a propeller-driven engine. Since there was no engine light enough or powerful enough, Cayley designed his own. It was an internal combustion engine which would use "oil of tar," or gasoline, as we now call it. But the fuel was too costly and Cayley was forced to abandon his engine. It was not until almost a hundred years later that such an engine was successfully built.

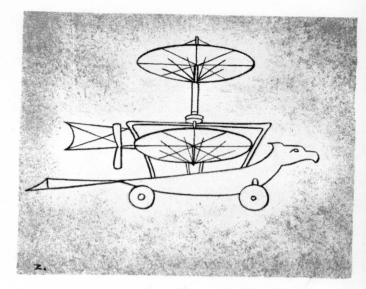

Sir George Cayley, father of aeronautics, built a successful glider in 1804, but he was unable to build a powered aircraft. His designs, however, were good.

Powered flight really started with William Henson and John Stringfellow. Using Cayley's principles, these two

When did the first powered airplane fly?

Englishmen designed an *aerial steam carriage* in 1842. Many of their ideas were practical, but they, too, were ahead of their time — there was no adequate engine.

In 1848, Stringfellow, working alone, built a model 10 feet long with a batlike wing. It had an engine which weighed less than 9 pounds and powered two propellers. It made short, sustained flights, flying as much as 40 yards. It was only a model, but it was real, powered flight.

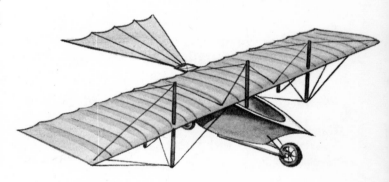

The immediate ancestor of the successful powered airplane was the glider. It is a

How does a glider fly?

heavier-than-air machine *without* an engine. The glider uses air currents to sustain its flight. In calm weather, it can be launched

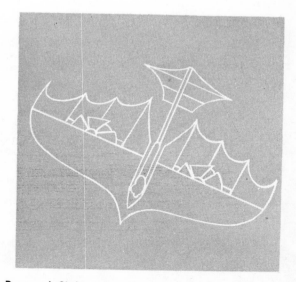

Powered flight came closer to reality with William Samuel Henson and John Stringfellow. They designed and flew the first powered models. But they were unable to build an engine to power a full-size plane.

from a high hilltop to obtain the needed forward thrust. The air rushing past its wings creates the necessary upward lift to counteract the gravitational force. The glider floats on the air and gradually descends to the ground.

In strong winds, the glider can be launched uphill so that it is picked up by the strong currents. It soars into the sky and continues to fly until the wind currents can no longer sustain it.

The greatest contribution in this field was made by Otto and Gustav Lilienthal. While still in high school in Germany, Otto built his first glider. It had wings that measured 6 by 3 feet each. In 1891, in Anklam, Germany, Otto made the first successful glider flight.

The brothers, noticing that birds took off *into* the wind, did the same with their gliders. They built many monoplane (single wing) and biplane (double wing) gliders and made over two thousand successful flights.

Perhaps Otto Lilienthal could have flown an airplane if a successful engine were available. In his attempt to develop such an engine, Otto lost his life. His experimental engine failed in flight and the airplane crashed.

Who made the first successful powered flight? Professor Langley, mathematician, physicist and Director of the Smithsonian Institution in Washington, D. C., was the last great air pioneer who failed to fly a plane. Using models, he supplied the answers to several problems which had to be solved before flying could be successful.

Early in the Spanish-American War, President McKinley asked Langley to develop a flying machine. Langley's assistant, Charles Manly, designed and built the first radial engine — the cylinders are built in a circle around the crankshaft. The engine used gasoline as fuel — it was Cayley's dream come true, almost a hundred years later.

Langley's *aerodrome* (AER-o-drome), as he called his plane, failed to fly on its second test on October 7, 1903. But some two months later, on December 17, 1903, at Kitty Hawk, North Carolina, the Wright brothers made the first successful flight.

Wilbur and Orville Wright were bicycle manufacturers from Dayton, Ohio, who built and flew gliders as early as 1900. After extensive work

The brothers Otto and Gustav Lilienthal paved the way for modern aviation. They built many gliders which flew successfully, and attempted powered flight. Otto was killed while testing a glider to which was attached a motor run by carbon dioxide.

on models, tested in wind tunnels, the Wright brothers designed and built their engine — a 4-cylinder model, weighing about 200 pounds, which developed 16 horsepower. They mounted this engine in a reinforced glider, and at Kitty Hawk, Orville Wright made four successful flights in one day. The first lasted only 12 seconds during which time the plane flew 120 feet. On the fourth flight the plane covered 852 feet and remained in the air for 59 seconds.

Despite its advanced engine, Samuel Langley's plane failed to fly. The gasoline engine, weighing less than three pounds per horsepower, was unequaled for twenty years.

How did early aviation progress?

The Wright brothers worked in Dayton for five years after their success at Kitty Hawk. In 1908, they developed a military airplane for the U. S. Army and in 1909, they demonstrated that a plane was capable of carrying a passenger. It flew at 40 miles per hour, carrying enough gasoline for a flight of 125 miles.

All over Europe and America, successful airplanes were demonstrated. In 1909, Louis Blériot flew across the English Channel. In that same year, the first international air meet was held at Rheims, France with thirty-eight airplanes participating. At that meet, Glenn H. Curtis, an American airplane designer and builder, established the speed record of 47.8 miles per hour. Hubert Latham, an Englishman, set the altitude record of 508 feet, while Henri Farman, a Frenchman, established the endurance record of 3 hours and 5 min-

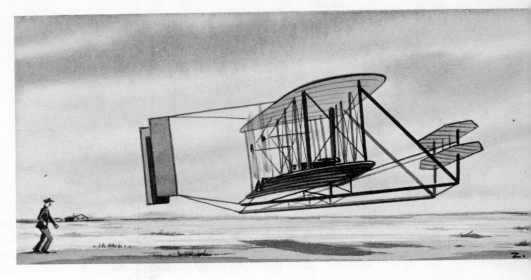

On December 17, 1903, at Kitty Hawk, North Carolina, the first heavier-than-air plane was flown by the Wrights.

Louis Blériot set a new record when, in 1909, he flew across the English Channel in this small plane.

The first plane to take off and land on a ship at sea was flown by Eugene Ely, an American (1910).

utes. The longest flight at the meet was 118 miles.

One year later, in 1910, Eugene Ely, an American pilot, demonstrated a flight which eventually led to aircraft carriers. His plane took off from the cruiser *U.S.S. Birmingham* and landed on the battleship *U.S.S. Pennsylvania*.

The outbreak of World War I spurred the development of the airplane. Although attention was concentrated on the plane as a military weapon, it helped to establish aviation, train pilots, foster aircraft manufacturing and increase the public's awareness of aviation's possibilities.

Many men took to flying. They bought surplus Government airplanes, and earned their living doing stunt flying and taking people up for short flights around airports. These men were the so-called "gypsies" and "barnstormers" who helped aviation to grow.

Glenn Curtis was not only a plane designer and pilot, but also a manufacturer. All his planes were named after birds—*Hawk, Eagle, Condor, Falcon* and *Robin*.

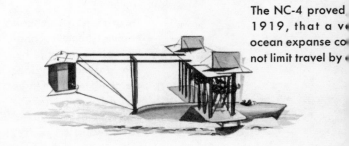

The NC-4 proved 1919, that a v ocean expanse co not limit travel by

In May 1919, the NC-4 made aviation

How did airplanes "shrink" the world? history by crossing the Atlantic. The Navy had three patrol bombers, flying boats which could take off and land only in water. Each plane carried a crew of five: two pilots, a radio operator, an engineer and a reserve engineer-pilot. Only the NC-4 completed the journey from Rockaway, Long Island to Plymouth, England, a distance of 3,936 miles. Some fifty destroyers lined the Atlantic to act as guides for the planes and to be ready to help any that were in distress. The total flying time was 52½ hours, not including the time necessary at the seven stops for refueling and repairs.

In 1924, the Army sent its Douglas biplane bombers on a flight around the world. Four planes left Seattle, Washington on April 6. On September 28, only two — the *Chicago* and the *New Orleans* — returned. They had crossed twenty-eight countries, covered 26,345

Some 33 hours and 30 minutes after he took off from Roosevelt Field in Long Island, Lindbergh landed his *Spirit of St. Louis* at Le Bourget, an airfield outside of Paris.

Two Douglas World Cruisers carried their Army flight crews in the first round-the-world flight in 1924.

During parts of their trip, the landing wheels were replaced by pontoons.

miles, and crossed the Pacific for the first time. The actual flying time was about 15½ days.

The race from New York to Paris was

Who made the first nonstop solo flight across the Atlantic? spurred by a $25,000 prize which Raymond Orteig, French-born owner of a New York hotel, offered to the first one to make the flight nonstop. Although Orteig offered this money in 1919, it was not

until 1926 that Rene Founck, a famous French aviator of World War I, made the first try. His plane crashed at take-off.

Many others tried and failed. It was Captain Charles A. Lindbergh, a former mail pilot, Army officer and barnstormer, who finally claimed the prize. Financed by a group of St. Louis businessmen, Lindbergh had Ryan Aircraft of San Diego build a special monoplane with a Wright J-5 Whirlwind engine at a cost of $10,580. The builders at Ryan worked as many as eighteen hours a day to complete the plane in sixty days.

Lindbergh brought his plane, *The Spirit of St. Louis,* to Roosevelt Field, Long Island where, despite the fog and drizzle, he took off at 7:52 A.M. on May 20, 1927. To make room for extra gasoline, Lindbergh flew alone. To make the plane lighter, he carried no parachute and removed the radio and all other "surplus" equipment and charts.

Alone, with no radio, Lindbergh plowed through rain, sleet, fog and high winds across the Atlantic, flew over Ireland and England and on over France. He circled the Eiffel Tower and landed nearby at the airport of Le Bourget, on May 21 at 10:22 P.M., Paris time. He had flown over 3,600 miles in 33 hours and 30 minutes.

The "Lone Eagle," as Lindbergh was called, was greeted by large, enthusiastic crowds. He received wild welcomes everywhere he went. The world was talking about "Lucky Lindy" — and aviation.

FAMOUS FIRSTS IN EARLY AVIATION

The first air-mail service was established by the U. S. Post Office between New York and Washington, D. C. on May 15, 1918. Major Reuben Fleet piloted the first flight and Lieutenant George Boyle made the return flight.

* * *

The first nonstop transatlantic flight was made by Captain John Alcock and Lieutenant Arthur Brown of England in a Vickers-Vimy biplane on June 14, 1919. They flew from Newfoundland to Clifdon, Ireland in 16 hours and 12 minutes.

* * *

The first nonstop transcontinental flight from New York to San Diego was made by Lieutenants Oakley Kelly and John Macready in May, 1923. Their trip in a Fokker T-2 took 26 hours and 50 minutes.

* * *

The first airplane flight over the North Pole was made on May 9, 1926. Lieutenant Floyd Bennett piloted a trimotor Fokker, commanded by Commander Richard E. Byrd, from Spitzbergen, Norway. During the 15 hours, before the plane returned to its base, it flew over the Pole.

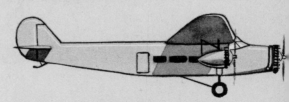

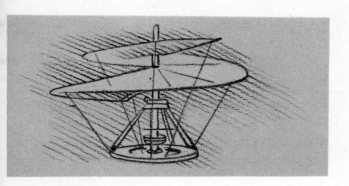

Da Vinci designed a helixpteron, the first helicopter.

The Launoy, or Chinese flying top, was the first successful model of a heavier-than-air machine that man built. It was the basis for the development of copters.

Flying in Any Direction

A helicopter can fly in any direction — straight up, straight down, forward, backward, sideways — and it can even stand still in mid-air. Furthermore, the helicopter can creep along a few inches above the ground or water, or it can climb thousands of feet into the sky and travel at over 100 miles per hour.

The fifteenth century genius, Leonardo da Vinci, not only de-

How did the helicopter originate?

signed a workable parachute and the ornithopter, but he also designed a very special flying machine. Overhead, it had a large screw-shaped propeller, which da Vinci hoped would screw into the air and lift the machine. He called this flying machine the *helixpteron* (hel-i-TER-on), which comes from the Greek *helix* (meaning "spiral") and *pteron* (meaning "wing").

For more than two hundred fifty years no one paid attention to this idea. But in 1783, the French naturalist Launoy "discovered" a Chinese flying top, a toy probably brought back from the Orient. The top was made of feathers, wood and string and it could fly straight up. It was the first man-made heavier-than-air object that could leave the ground on its own power.

This top inspired George Cayley and he built a similar one, but used tin for the blades instead of feathers. The Cayley top rose 90 feet into the air.

All you need in order to make a Cayley

How can you make a Cayley top?

top is a 6-inch model airplane propeller, an empty spool, a dowel that just about slides through the hole in the spool and a piece of string about 2 feet long.

Nail the propeller to one end of the dowel. Wind the string around the

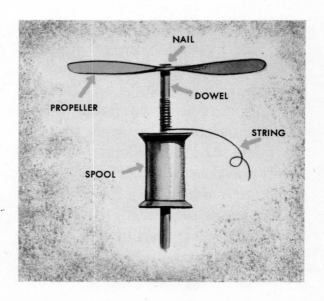

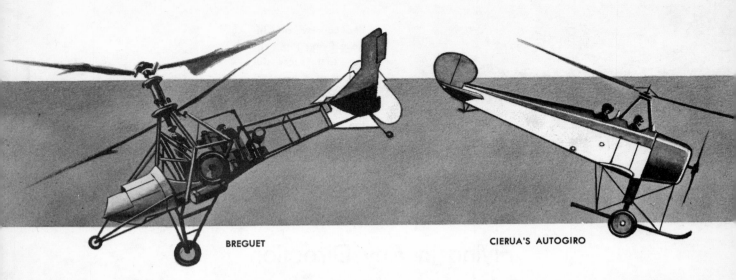

BREGUET

CIERUA'S AUTOGIRO

dowel, about an inch below the propeller. Then, slide the dowel into the spool. Hold the spool in one hand with the propeller pointing straight up. Pull the string hard and quickly with the other hand. The propeller spins and lifts the dowel straight into the air.

In 1878, Enrico Forlanini, using a powerful, tiny steam engine he designed and built, made a model helicopter. This steam-driven model hovered in the air at about 40 feet for 20 seconds. It provided positive proof that such a flying machine was possible.

Who were the early helicopter builders?

The first full-sized helicopter to fly was built by Louis Breguet in 1907. This plane rose some 5 feet off the ground, but it could not be controlled and was unstable. It was not until 1922 that Russian-born George de Bothezat built and flew a helicopter that was stable and controllable. His *Flying Octopus,* built as a military helicopter, was an enormous ship with four rotors or horizontal blades. Although it made over one hundred successful flights from McCook Field in the United States, it

was abandoned because it was too clumsy and complicated.

The *autogyro* (auto-GY-ro) is a hybrid, a combination of an airplane and helicopter. Its Spanish inventor, Juan de la Cierva, used a small biplane and attached a set of whirling blades on top of the plane. There was no engine to work the top blades. They turned as the air from the propeller rushed passed them.

How does an autogyro fly?

The turning of the rotary blades gave the plane extra lift or upward pull. For this reason, it was possible for the plane to take off at a slower engine speed and get into the air in less time. It appeared to jump into the air at take-off.

The autogyro's whirling blades turned only when the plane's propeller was spinning and, therefore, it hovered in the air. The only advantage of the autogyro was its ability to get into the air quickly at a lower engine speed. Although the autogyro has disappeared from the sky, the development of flexible rotary blades by Juan de la Cierva helped make it possible to build truly successful helicopters.

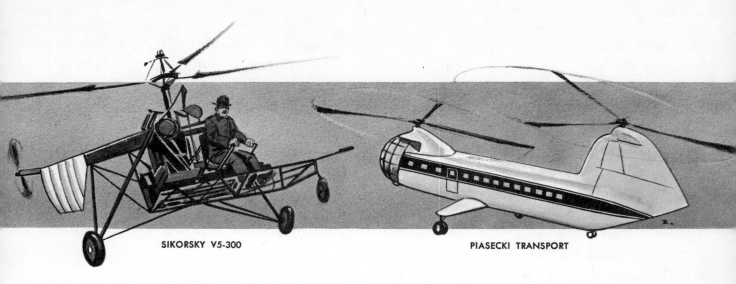

SIKORSKY V5-300

PIASECKI TRANSPORT

One man stands out in the history of
Who perfected the helicopter? helicopters — Igor Sikorsky. As a young man in Kiev, Russia, he built a model helicopter in 1910. He continued to study the experiments of others and in 1939, working in the United States, he decided to try again.

For months, he worked on "Igor's Nightmare," as many people called his helicopter. He conducted many experiments and in May, 1940, he tried his first free flight. It was an overwhelming success compared with anything that preceded it. His ship could fly up, down, backward, sideways, and could hover in the air. But his ship had difficulty in flying forward. Additional work solved this problem and he started to produce workable helicopters.

World War II spurred the development of helicopters and in 1943, eighteen-year-old Stanley Hiller, Jr. designed and built the first coaxial helicopter. He used one engine to turn both rotors.

The helicopter now has many uses. It is used to spray chemicals over crops to protect them from insects, to fight forest fires, to carry mail, to inspect power lines and pipe lines in rugged mountain country. It is also used in land- and sea-rescue work, by cowboys on very large ranches, and even acts as a "bus" between airports.

The rotor blades over the helicopter lift
How does the helicopter fly? the ship and make it fly. The blades act somewhat like the wings of an airplane. The pilot of a helicopter can tilt these blades — this tilt is called *pitch*. Tilting the moving blades creates lift. If you have ever flown a kite, you know how this works. The kite is tilted in the air, held in that position by the string you hold in your hand. The moving air passes the tilted kite, lifts it and keeps it flying. But if you let go of the string, the kite is no longer tilted, and it will glide down to the ground.

To climb into the air, the pilot tilts the moving blades and the helicopter goes straight up. When he wants to come down, he decreases the tilt, or pitch, of the blades. This decreases the lift, and gravity brings the ship down. If he wants to hover or stand still in the air, he sets the pitch of the blades so that the upward lift equals the pull

23

toward the ground. Now, picture these moving blades as a saucer. You can tilt the entire saucer in any direction. It is through this tilting that the pilot can make the plane go forward, backward or sideways.

There is a smaller set of blades near the tail of the helicopter, nicknamed a "pinwheel." These blades also revolve and their pitch can be changed as well. By controlling their pitch, the pilot can keep the ship straight or make right and left turns.

Modern aviation has made it possible
How do the modern ornithopters fly? for man to fly like a bird. A miniature helicopter is capable of carrying one man. He can fly straight up, sideways, forward, backward, downward or hover in the air. The personal *whirlywings* have been used experimentally by the U. S. Army for its scouts.

This is a U. S. Army craft — a whirlywing.

The *aerocycle* is another version of a one-man helicopter. This experimental model, also used by the Army, is somewhat larger than a *whirlywing* and the man stands on top of the cycle to fly it through the air.

Another small, one-man flying machine is the *flying platform*. It is shaped like a large doughnut and has a fan in

FLYING PLATFORM

the center. This fan lifts and propels the platform on which the man stands. The pilot's "leaning" controls the horizontal flight of this craft.

Picture an airplane, higher than a three-
What is VTOL? story building, standing on its tail. The propeller starts turning and soon the plane goes straight up into the air. Once the

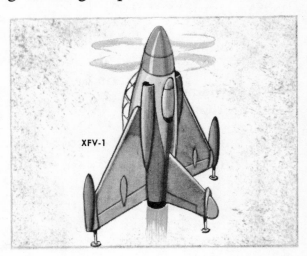

XFV-1

pilot gets up as high as he wants to go, he straightens out the plane and it flies like any ordinary airplane. Such planes as the Lockheed XFV-1 and the Convair XFY-1, often called "flying pogo sticks," are VTOL aircraft. VTOL means "vertical take-off and landing."

Although these planes are like conventional, horizontal flying craft, they act like helicopters in some ways. Not only can they take off and land vertically, but they can hover in the air as well. These experimental planes can take off and land from practically any place — the top of a building, the deck of a ship or in rugged mountain country studded with trees. Once aloft, they are high-speed aircraft and can exceed 500 miles per hour.

Theory and Facts of Flight

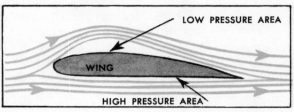

As the air rushes past the wing, or airfoil, it flows above and below the airfoil. The shape of the airfoil causes the air to travel a greater distance over the top of the foil. This results in a lowering of air pressure, which creates an upward lift on the airfoil.

Why does an airplane fly? About forty years before the American Revolution, a Swiss scientist, Daniel Bernoulli, discovered that in any moving fluid the pressure is lowest where the speed is greatest. The air about us acts like a fluid and if we can increase the speed of air over a surface, such as a wing, the pressure should decrease and the wing should rise.

In actual practice, the wing of an airplane is shaped somewhat like a bow — the upper surface is curved while the lower part is straight. Since the air has to travel a greater distance over the top part of the wing, it must travel at a faster speed. As a result, the pressure is lower above the wing than below it and the wing rises, or *lifts,* into the air.

When an airplane flies horizontally, its propeller must do two things. First, it must keep the plane from falling and, second, it must overcome the friction of the air in order to pull the plane forward. The turning propeller increases the speed of the air over the wings. According to the Bernoulli principle, this creates *lift* — the upward pressure on the wing. Lift overcomes *gravity* — the downward pressure created by the weight of the plane.

The propeller slices through the air in the same way that a screw cuts into wood, and pulls the plane forward. This forward motion of the propeller is called *thrust.* It counteracts the *drag* of the atmosphere, the force that resists forward motion.

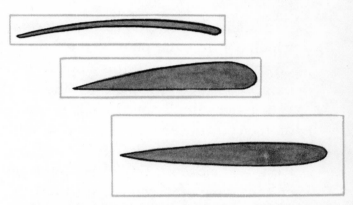

Airfoil cross sections, top to bottom: Design used by Wright brothers; "high-light" wing used on small planes; "high-speed" wing used by commercial liners.

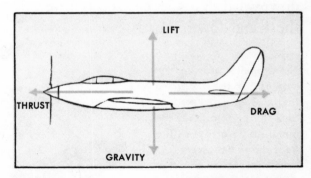

These four forces act upon a plane while in flight.

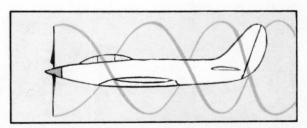

The propeller, called airscrews in England, provides the forward pulling or lifting power of an airplane.

An airplane, like any moving object

What makes an airplane go up and down? following the basic laws of physics, tends to continue in a straight line unless some force is exerted to change its direction. The speed at which the engine turns the propeller is governed by the *throttle*. Opening the throttle increases the air speed and lifts the plane higher.

Equally important is the *elevator* which controls the plane's upward and downward movement. It is a horizontal, hinged surface attached to the tail. When the pilot applies back pressure on the control stick, or column, the elevator is tilted upward. The air, striking the raised elevator, forces the tail down and the wing upward. The thrust of the propeller pulls the plane upward. Conversely, when the pilot pushes the control stick forward, the elevator is tilted downward. This forces the tail up and the wing down.

Two parts of an airplane control its

How does an airplane turn? turns to the right and left. The *rudder,* a vertical surface that is hinged to the tail, swings the tail to the right or left just in the same way as a section of the tail swings up or down. On the ground, it is used to make the plane turn just as a rudder of a boat does. In the air, however, the major purpose of the rudder is *not* to make the plane turn, but to assist the plane in entering and recovering from a turn.

The *ailerons,* small sections of the rear edge of the wing, near the tips, are hinged and are so connected that as one rises, the other lowers. This action tends to raise one wing and lower the other.

When the aileron on the right wing is lowered, the right wing rises and the plane will be tilted, or *banked,* to the left. The lifting force on the right wing is no longer completely upward — part of the force is pulling the plane to the left. This, in combination with the rudder, produces a left turn; that is, the plane is "lifted" around the turn.

The propeller provides the power for the forward thrust. The elevators enable the pilot to make the plane go up or down. The flaps aid in the ascent and help provide a smoother descent. The ailerons and rudder help the plane to turn left and right.

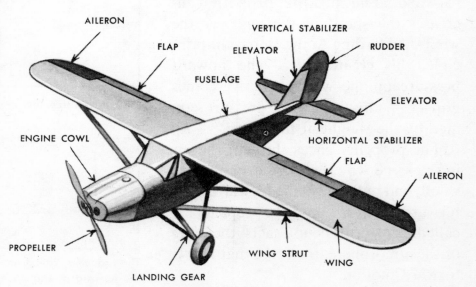

AILERON

FLAP

FUSELAGE

VERTICAL STABILIZER

ELEVATOR

RUDDER

ELEVATOR

HORIZONTAL STABILIZER

ENGINE COWL

FLAP

AILERON

PROPELLER

WING STRUT

WING

LANDING GEAR

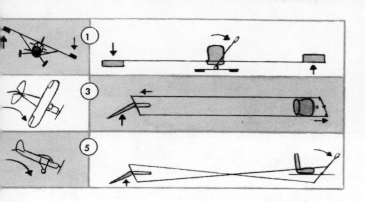

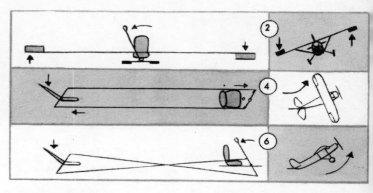

HOW TO FLY AN AIRPLANE

AILERONS (FRONT VIEW)	RUDDER (TOP VIEW)	ELEVATORS (SIDE VIEW)
1. LEFT STICK	3. RIGHT RUDDER	5. FORWARD STICK
2. RIGHT STICK	4. LEFT RUDDER	6. BACKWARD STICK

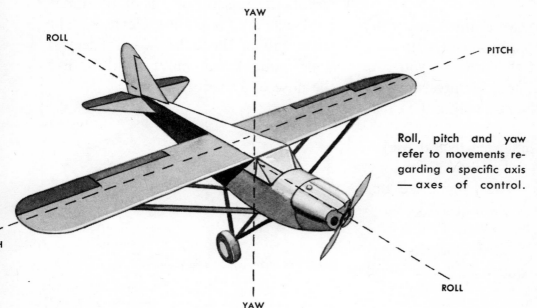

Roll, pitch and yaw refer to movements regarding a specific axis — axes of control.

How can you demonstrate *lift*? Take a piece of paper about 2 inches wide and about 5 inches long. Fold it an inch from the end. Hold the paper with your forefinger and thumb so that the fold is about an inch or two from your mouth. Blow with all your might over the top of the paper.

What happened? The paper moves up or *lifts*. By increasing the speed of the air over the top of the paper, you have reduced the pressure, causing the paper to rise.

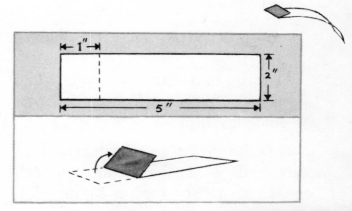

You can demonstrate lift, caused by the Bernoulli effect, on the upper surface of a piece of paper (right).

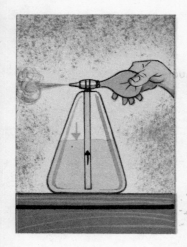
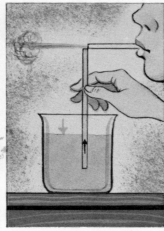

You can demonstrate this same principle with a simple atomizer. Blowing across the top of the tube — you can use a straw — reduces the pressure and causes the liquid to rise within the tube.

How can you demonstrate the working of an elevator?

Take a 3 by 5 index card and fold a 1-inch section along the long edge upward at a 45-degree angle. Paste the card, along its short center line, to a piece of balsa wood

about 10 inches long. Balance the wood with the attached card on a round pencil, like a seesaw. Mark this "balance" point and push a straight pin through the balsa so that it is parallel to the card.

Hold the pin lightly between the thumb and forefinger of both hands. Hold the balsa wood in front of your mouth with the card farthest away. Now when you blow with all your might, the raised portion of the index card acts like a plane's elevator. The front end of the balsa wood (nearest your mouth) will move upward, like the nose of a plane.

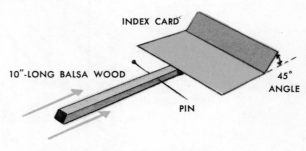

INDEX CARD

10"-LONG BALSA WOOD

PIN

45° ANGLE

DIRECTION FROM WHICH YOU BLOW

WHAT DO THE INSTRUMENTS TELL THE PILOT?

Here are only a few of the more important instruments which a pilot uses to guide his airplane:

Oil Pressure Gauge indicates the pressure of the oil in the engine. The dial is colored so that it is easier for the pilot to instantly spot any danger.

Oil Temperature Gauge tells the temperature of the oil in the engine.

Rate-of-Climb Indicator tells the pilot the speed at which his plane is climbing

or dropping. The indicator is at zero when the plane is flying level.

Air Speed Indicator notes how fast the plane is moving through the air. Four colors are used for greater safety. Red is used to show maximum speed at which the plane can fly. Yellow shows a caution range — speeds approaching maximum speed. Heavy blue is used for normal cruising speeds. Light blue is used to show landing speed.

Turn-and-Bank Indicator is actually two separate instruments. The curved glass tube with a metal ball in liquid, the bank indicator, located near the bottom of the instrument, shows whether the plane is tilted to the right or left. The turn indicator shows the direction in which the nose of the plane is headed — to the left, straight ahead or to the right.

Instrument Landing System Indicator helps the pilot land his plane when the airfield is covered by fog or very low clouds. When the two pointers line up with the white circles on the dial, the plane is directly on path approaching the runway for a perfect landing.

Fuel Gauge indicates how much gasoline the plane has in its tank.

Tachometer tells the pilot how his motor is doing. It indicates the number of revolutions of the engine or the speed at which the propellers are turning.

Altimeter shows the height of the plane above the ground. There are three pointers — the smallest shows height in tens of thousands of feet above the ground; the medium-sized pointer shows height in thousands of feet; and the longest pointer shows height in hundreds and parts of hundreds of feet. The altimeter pictured here shows an altitude, or height, of 14,750 feet.

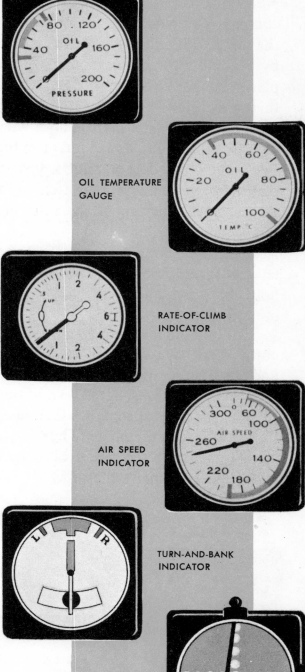

OIL PRESSURE GAUGE

OIL TEMPERATURE GAUGE

RATE-OF-CLIMB INDICATOR

AIR SPEED INDICATOR

TURN-AND-BANK INDICATOR

INSTRUMENT LANDING SYSTEM INDICATOR

ALTIMETER

TACHOMETER

FUEL GAUGE

Directional Gyro and Magnetic Compass are used to guide the plane. The magnetic compass acts like any regular compass you have seen — it points to the north. The directional gyro is used by the pilot to set his course. If the plane changes direction, the gyro shows this to the pilot.

Artificial Horizon helps a pilot when he is flying at night, in a cloud or in fog. During a clear day, a pilot keeps his plane straight and level by watching the horizon. At other times, he must use this instrument.

Drift Indicator is usually installed level with the floor. It shows the pilot how the wind might be blowing him off course.

In multi-engine, conventional aircraft, there is a separate oil pressure and oil temperature indicator and a tachometer for each engine. In addition, there is generally a separate fuel gauge for each tank in the plane. Thus, if you were to look at the panel of a large four-engine airliner which has six fuel

tanks, you would see seventeen more instruments than you see here. Furthermore, there is an identical set of dials for the co-pilot in addition to the pilot, and on some planes a third set of dials is used for the navigator-engineer.

Highways of the Air

There are thousands of airports of many different kinds throughout the world. In the United States, the Civil Aeronautics Administration (CAA) classifies the airports according to the length of their runways. An airport with a runway of 1,500 to 2,300 feet is classified as a personal airport and is used only by small, light, private planes.

DIRECTIONAL GYRO AND
MAGNETIC COMPASS

DRIFT INDICATOR

ARTIFICIAL HORIZON

Airports range from the small grass fields for two- and four-passen-

ger planes to the very large fields with concrete runways that handle the large commercial jet airliners.

Airports where large domestic passenger airliners can land and take off must have runways of 6,000 to 7,000 feet. To meet the needs of today's large jetliners, some airports have runways of 10,000 feet or more, or about two miles.

In the air between the airports are

What are the airways? *airways,* or roads, through the sky along which the planes travel. Because of the many planes flying overhead, both during the day and night, it is necessary to set up rules for the road just as we have traffic rules for the cars on the streets.

Except when taking off or landing, airplanes must fly at least 500 feet above the ground. Over cities and other

congested areas, the planes often have to fly 1,000 or even 2,000 feet above the ground.

The route a plane takes is determined by the CAA which controls all air traffic. At major airports, there are men sitting before air maps, radios and control boards, and they keep track of every plane as it plows through the skies.

Specific airways have been established to prevent planes from colliding in the air. All eastbound flights — planes flying from west to east — fly at *odd* thousand-foot levels, plus 500 feet, above sea level. Thus, a plane flying from Los Angeles to New York could fly at 15,500 feet. Westbound flights, on the other hand, fly at *even* thousand-foot levels, plus 500 feet, above sea level.

WHICH PLANE HAS THE RIGHT OF WAY?

Aircraft have rules that govern the right of way in the sky.

All flying craft have to give the right of way to a balloon.

Airplanes and airships have to give a glider the right of way.

An airplane must give an airship the right of way.

*   *   *

If two planes are flying so that their paths might cross, the plane to the right of the pilot has the right of way.

*   *   *

Should two planes be approaching head-on, both pilots must shift their planes to the right. As they pass, the planes must be at least 500 feet apart.

The same plane going from New York to Los Angeles could fly at 14,500 feet.

During a clear, sunny day — or Class C

How do air markers help pilots to fly?

weather according to the Air Weather Bureau — planes can fly by contact; that is, the pilot can see the ground and identify his route. There are various markers along the route on the ground. These markers also appear on special flight maps which the pilot carries with him just as we carry a road map in a car.

The air markers indicate location, have arrows pointing to the nearest air-

port and other identifying information. The markers are painted on highways, roofs of barns and factories, and the sides of high buildings such as grain elevators. They are also set in stone on mountains or in fields.

In addition to the visible markers, there is also radio contact. The CAA operates many radio stations throughout the country. By picking up different stations, the pilot can determine his exact position over the ground.

During the night, when it is clear, the pilot can spot visible ground markers, some of which are illuminated, special air beacons (similar to lights from a lighthouse) and airport lights and beacons.

Look into the cockpit of an airplane

How do pilots fly in all types of weather?

and you will see a maze of dials, knobs, switches and levers. These instruments and controls help the pilot at take-off, when he guides the plane safely through the airways and when he lands. Today's plane can land even when the pilot cannot see the airport.

The Instrument Landing System (ILS) is used when the airport's *ceiling* (the height from the ground to the clouds above) is too low for the pilot to land by sight. Through the use of electronic equipment, the pilot can "see" through the fog, rain, sleet and dark. A special instrument on his flight panel helps him align his airplane directly with the airport's runway. The instrument also shows him if he is too high or too low as he approaches.

Radar is also used to help pilots fly

through foul weather and to land safely. The major airports use Air Surveillance Radar (ASR) with which they can pinpoint the exact position in the sky of any plane within 60 miles of the airport. Some of the newer *blind landing* techniques (when the pilot cannot see the airport landing strip) involve automatic controls. The pilot sets the plane on special electronic instruments, and a ground controller, using radar, actually lands the plane.

Faster Than Sound

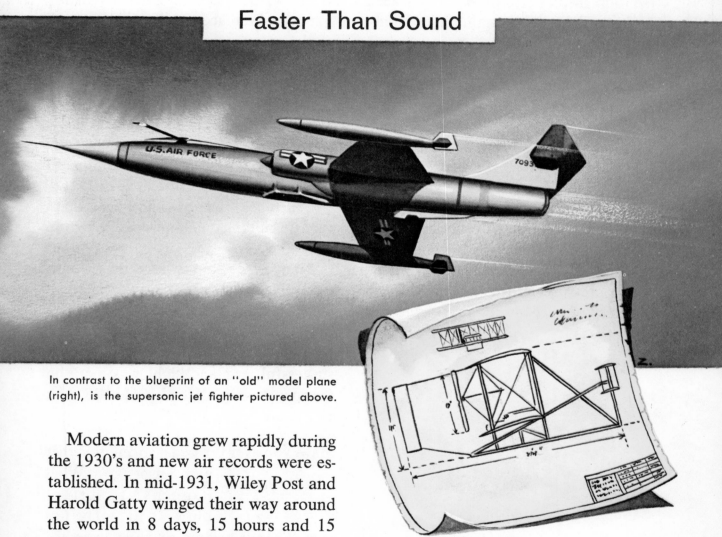

In contrast to the blueprint of an "old" model plane (right), is the supersonic jet fighter pictured above.

Modern aviation grew rapidly during the 1930's and new air records were established. In mid-1931, Wiley Post and Harold Gatty winged their way around the world in 8 days, 15 hours and 15 minutes. Two years later, Wiley Post set out by himself in his plane, the *Winnie Mae,* and made the same earth-circling trip in 7 days, 8 hours and 49 minutes. During this flight, he used two new aviation instruments — the radio compass and a robot or automatic pilot.

It has been said that the world was put on wings when the Douglas DC-3 was introduced in 1936. Until that time, the airlines used small planes, such as the Fokker trimotor and Ford trimotor. Each carried only eight people and reached top speeds of about 100 miles an hour. The DC-3 carried twenty-one passengers in addition to a crew of three, and it could fly at 180 miles per hour. This "workhorse of the airlines" helped to build air passenger travel in the United States.

The outbreak of World War II in September, 1939 signaled a new era in aviation history. Emphasis was placed on faster fighter planes, on larger bombers that could fly higher, and on troop transports that could carry more men and fly farther. World War II saw the first jet planes in real action.

The idea of jet power, or propulsion,

When were jets first used?

goes back to early history. The Greek mathematician, Hero, who lived in Alexandria about 130 B.C., is credited with being the first to build a jet engine. He converted steam pressure into jet action with an "engine" of his own design. It consisted

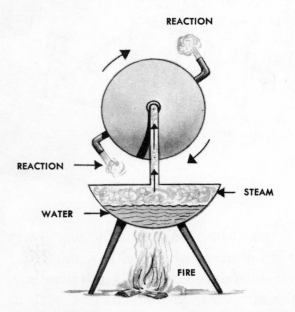

The "aeoliphile" was built by Hero of Alexandria.

of a hollow metal sphere which was mounted so that it could spin freely. The steam inside the sphere escaped through small nozzles, causing the sphere to spin. This engine was a scientific toy and was never put to use.

The jet principle was put to work during the Middle Ages in Europe. The *smoke-jack,* which some claim da Vinci invented, was used to turn a roasting spit in a fireplace. The turning action of the spit was produced by a fan in the chimney. The hot air passing up the chimney turned the fan.

In 1629, Giovanni Branca perfected a steam turbine using the jet principle to operate a milling machine. He used steam, which passed through a pipe, to turn a paddle-wheel similar to our modern turbines. The paddle-wheel operated the milling machine, crushing grain into flour.

Many other men worked on jet-powered machines over the years, and in 1926 an English scientist, Dr. Griffiths, proposed the use of jet-powered gas turbines to power an airplane. The first successful jet-plane flight was made in Germany when a Heinkel He-178 took to the air on August 27, 1939.

Have you ever pressed a spring together

How does a jet fly?

and let it go? What happens? It springs back to its original size. The air around us behaves in the same way. When you compress air, it tries to escape and expand to its original volume. When you heat air, it expands, and also tries to escape. Compressing and heating air give the jet engine its power.

If you take an inflated balloon and let it go, the air inside the balloon will escape. As it rushes out, the balloon "flies" through the air. This illustrates the principle which makes the jet fly. It is an example of Newton's third law of motion: "For every action, there is an equal and opposite reaction." As the air rushes out the back, the balloon goes forward.

The balloon's activity is a form of jet propulsion.

There are several types of jet engines and all work on the same principle. A jet plane needs no propeller since it uses air to give it forward motion or thrust. The most common type of jet engine is the turbojet.

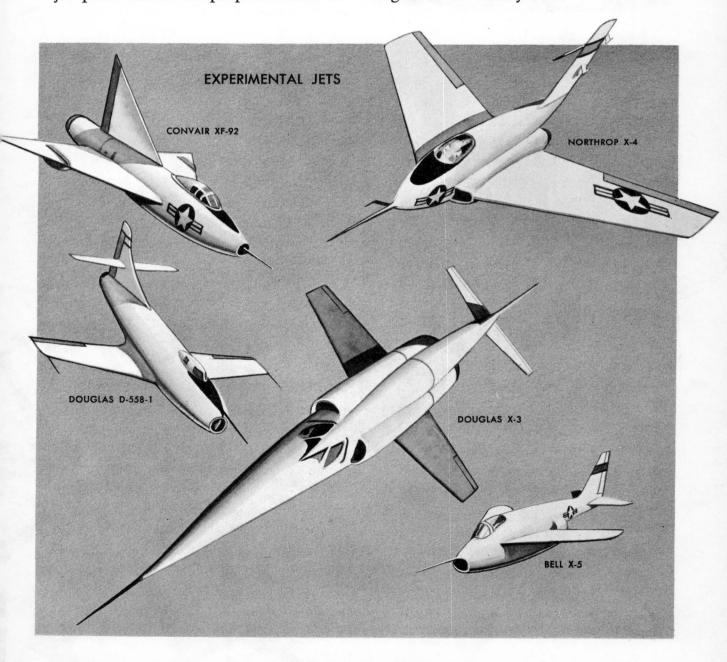

EXPERIMENTAL JETS

CONVAIR XF-92

NORTHROP X-4

DOUGLAS D-558-1

DOUGLAS X-3

BELL X-5

RAMJET AND PULSEJET

The *ramjet* is the simplest of all jet engines. It has no moving parts. The air is compressed by the forward motion of the plane. The plane has to be in motion *before* the ramjet works. Therefore, a plane with a ramjet engine has to be launched in the air by a "mother ship."

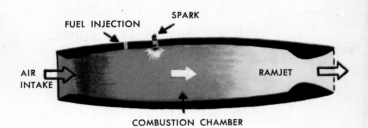

The *pulsejet* is also a simple jet engine. It has only one moving part, an inlet valve which controls the amount of air entering the engine. It was first used during World War II to power the V-1 flying bombs which the Germans rocketed into London, England.

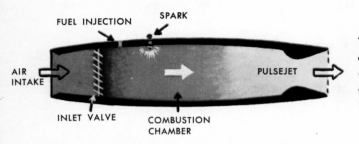

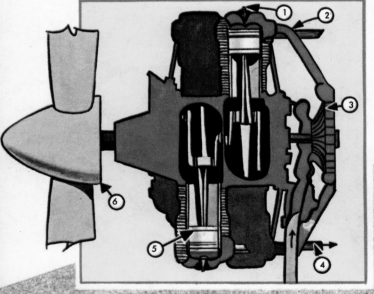

A reciprocating engine: (1) spark plug; (2) cylinder inlet; (3) shaft-driven supercharger; (4) cylinder exhaust; (5) piston; and (6) propeller.

Super aircraft require special aircraft facilities. One modern structure (below) is already built and in operation at Idlewild in N. Y.

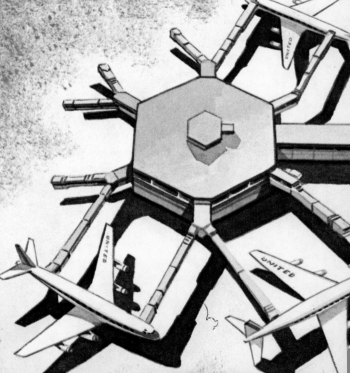

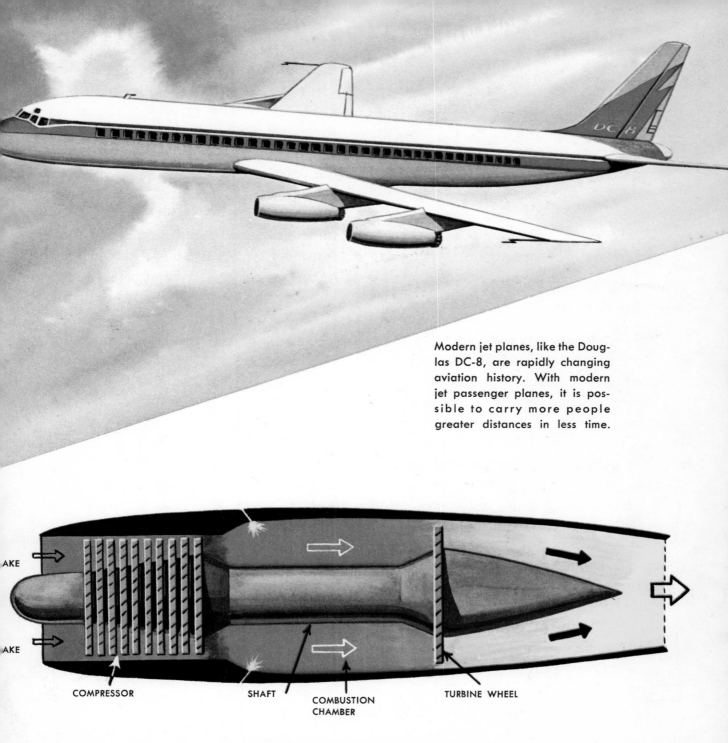

Modern jet planes, like the Douglas DC-8, are rapidly changing aviation history. With modern jet passenger planes, it is possible to carry more people greater distances in less time.

COMPRESSOR   SHAFT   COMBUSTION CHAMBER   TURBINE WHEEL

HOW A TURBOJET WORKS

1. Air is sucked into the engine through the front intake. The compressor, acting like a large fan, compresses the air and forces it through ducts, or tubes, to the combustion chamber.

2. In the combustion chamber, fuel is sprayed into the compressed air and ignited. The resulting hot gases expand rapidly and, with terrific force, blast their way out of the rear of the engine. This jet blast gives the engine and plane its forward thrust.

3. As the hot gases rush out of the engine, they pass through a set of blades, the turbine wheel. These blades react like a windmill and turn the main engine shaft, which operates the front compressor.

4. Some engines, designed to give extra pushing power, have an afterburner attached to the engine. This is a long tail cone in which more fuel is sprayed and burned, just before the gases pass through the rear exhaust.

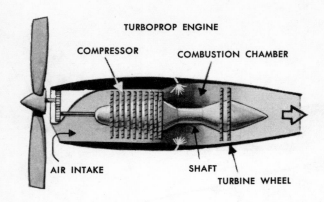

TURBOPROP ENGINE

COMPRESSOR COMBUSTION CHAMBER

AIR INTAKE SHAFT TURBINE WHEEL

A *turboprop* is a jet engine connected to

Why do they use turboprops?

a conventional propeller. It combines the advantages of a gas turbine jet with those of a propeller. During take-off and low speeds, the propeller produces higher forward thrust. During landing, the propeller creates greater drag, enabling the plane to take off and land in shorter distances than a turbojet. However, the gas turbine jet is lightweight as compared with a conventional plane's piston motor and is without vibration in flight.

A turboprop, or *propjet* as it is also called, cannot fly as fast or as high as a turbojet. Turbojets are particularly suited for high-speed and high-altitude flights. On the other hand, propjets are more efficient at moderate altitudes than conventional piston-engine planes.

Have you ever noticed that during a

What is the sound barrier?

lightning storm you can see the flash of lightning before you hear the thunder? This is because light travels faster than sound. The speed of sound in freezing air (32°F.) is about 1,090 feet per second or 743 miles per hour. The speed of sound increases as the temperature rises, about a foot a second faster for each degree. At 68°F.,

the speed of sound in air is about 1,130 feet per second or 765 miles per hour.

Sound travels through the air in waves similar to those produced when you drop a stone into a pond. One of the people who studied sound and air waves was an Austrian professor of physics, Ernest Mach. About 1870, he photographed cannon shells flying through the air in order to discover what happens to an object as it speeds through the air. He found that the moving object produced *shock waves*. The object pushes against the molecules in the air. As one molecule is pushed, it in turn pushes the others near it. Imagine a long line of boys standing one behind the other. The last boy in the line gets pushed. As he moves forward, he pushes the boy in front of him. This happens all the way down the line. This is how sound and shock waves are produced.

As the speed of a plane approaches the speed of sound, it is pushing rapidly against the molecules in the air and creating shock waves. As the plane reaches the same speed as sound, these waves pile up and form an invisible barrier. When the plane exceeds the speed of sound, it must "crash" through

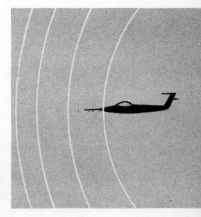

As the plane goes through the air, it creates sound waves. The plane itself displaces air about it as it speeds forward.

this barrier. As it does, it creates a thunderlike sound. You will see the plane before you hear its motor, just as you see lightning before you hear the thunder.

Slow-flying planes were never affected by air waves.

How did the sound barrier change the shape of planes?

As planes began to fly higher and faster, some pilots found that they encountered difficulties — the planes vibrated fiercely and the pilots couldn't operate the controls. What these pilots encountered was *wave drag;* that is, the piling-up of air in front of the plane — the sound barrier. Scientists and airmen studied this effect on planes and soon recognized what was happening.

To honor the man who first explored this subject scientifically, we measure the speed of a plane or rocket in *Mach numbers.* Aeronautical engineers use Mach 1 as equal to 680 miles per hour, the speed of sound at about 35,000 feet and higher, where the temperature is 50° or lower. Mach 2 equals twice the speed of sound or 1,360 miles per hour.

They found that the shock waves which caused wave drag were shaped

like a cone. If the plane has long wings, it tends to spin more easily. As a result, jet planes, designed to fly faster than sound, have shorter wings set farther back along the sides of the body.

Scientists have studied sound waves and plane speeds in special wind tunnels using model planes, and thus, have helped engineers to develop better planes.

As planes climbed higher into the air,

Why do planes fly in the jet stream?

meteorologists (weather men) and pilots discovered fast-moving "rivers of air" between 35,000 and 55,000 feet above the earth. These rivers generally flow in an east-west direction and reach speeds as high as 450 miles per hour. Since the jet planes were the first to

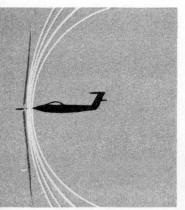

As the plane's speed is increased, approaching at the speed of sound, it is increasing the compression of the sound waves.

As the speed of the plane exceeds that of the waves it created, it then plunges headlong through the sound barrier.

39

reach such high altitudes, these "rivers" became known as the *jet stream*.

A plane flying in the same direction as the jet stream is carried along in much the same way as you are carried by a strong wind when you are walking with it on a very windy day. A plane flying 600 miles per hour with the jet stream traveling 300 miles per hour, is actually traveling 900 miles an hour over the earth. The jet stream helps conserve fuel and shorten flying time.

Revolutions in jet plane design are already taking place. One of the ships that North American Aviation is building is the B-70, half plane and half spaceship. This versatile craft, with a 156-foot pencil-thin body, is planned as a nuclear bomber with a range of 7,000 miles. As a passenger ship, it could carry 150

What will future jet planes be like?

people at over 2,000 miles per hour, and fly nonstop from San Francisco to London.

Another remarkable change is the development of an airbreathing aircraft wing by Dr. Werner Pfenninger. As the conventional aircraft wing slices through the air at supersonic speeds, the air around the wing becomes choppy or turbulent. This turbulence creates a drag on the wing, causing the plane to slow up. With the new wing design, there will be a smooth flow of air over and under the wing. This smoother flight will require less fuel so that planes will be able to fly about fifty per cent farther without refueling. Two pilot models of this type of aircraft are being built by Northrop Corporation under Dr. Pfenninger's guidance. If an air-inhaling system is also installed in the body of the plane, then its range might be doubled.

Airplanes of the future, speeding over 2,000 miles per hour, will look more like rockets than today's planes.

RECENT AVIATION HISTORY

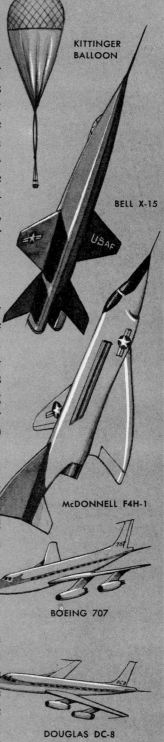

KITTINGER
BALLOON

BELL X-15

McDONNELL F4H-1

BOEING 707

DOUGLAS DC-8

GYRODYNE
ROTORCYCLE

Captain Joseph W. Kittinger, Jr., a thirty-one-year-old United States Air Force officer, soared nearly 103,000 feet above the New Mexico desert in an open-gondola balloon on August 16, 1960. He exceeded the old record set by Lieutenant Colonel David G. Simons, using a closed-gondola balloon, by some 500 feet.

After reaching the record height, Kittinger plunged toward the earth. He set a new world's record for free fall (jumping with a parachute closed). He plunged some 17 miles in 4 minutes and 38 seconds. Upon reaching about 17,500 feet, he opened his parachute and descended the remainder of his trip in 8 minutes and 30 seconds.

A new height-record for a balloon was set May 4, 1961 by Navy Commanders Malcolm Ross and Victor Prather. Their helium-filled balloon, with an aluminum-framed gondola, soared to 113,000 feet. Prather was killed during the helicopter rescue.

* * *

In 1959, the experimental military plane, the X-15, made its first free flight. At that time it reached an air speed of about 1,300 miles per hour — and exceeded an altitude of 50,000 feet.

* * *

During the spring of 1961, the X-15 set new records for experimental aircraft. It reached an altitude of 169,600 feet, more than 32 miles above the earth.

* * *

On April 21, 1961, Major Robert M. White of the Air Force set a new world speed record of 3,140 miles per hour in an X-15 rocket plane. The plane was released from a B-52 and achieved the record speed at an altitude of 80,000 feet above the earth.

* * *

In December, 1959, Major Joseph W. Rogers set the world's speed record for conventional jet aircraft for a straightaway course of 1,525 miles per hour. Within a year, on October 4, 1960, Commander John F. Davis of the United States Navy, flying a McDonnell F4H-1 *Phantom II* fighter, set the new world's speed record for a circular course, reaching 1,390.21 miles per hour.

* * *

In 1958, the first commercial jetliner, the Boeing 707, took to the air flying passengers for the airlines. Within the year, in 1959, the airlines also started using the Douglas DC-8. Both jetliners have cruising speeds of about 615 miles per hour and have a normal range of 1,750 miles with full pay-load.

* * *

Jetliners have set many new world speed records. One of the most outstanding has been a United Air Lines DC-8, which flew from Denver to New York City in 3 hours and 31 minutes, at an average air speed of 570 miles per hour.

* * *

Since the days of Daedalus, man has sought to fly with his "own wings." So far, the nearest man has come to this dream has been the one-man helicopter. The Gyrodyne YRON-1 *Rotorcycle* is now in full production for both the United States Navy and the Marine Corps. This small helicopter carries one man easily and can carry heavy loads in addition. It is now being used for map plotting and military observation, and will be used for anti-submarine missions by the United States Navy.

Rockets, Missiles and Satellites

How were rockets first used? Some historians believe that the Chinese used rockets, similar to our large firecrackers, at about the same time that the ancient Egyptians were building the Great Pyramids. They attached the rockets to arrows to make them fly farther. We do know that in A.D. 1232, during the Mongolian siege of the city of Kaifêng, the Chinese used *fei-i-ho-chien* (sticks of flying fire) to defend themselves. In fourteenth-century Europe, military rockets were used to set fire to cities and terrorize the enemy.

One of the most famous early uses of military rockets was at the Battle of Fort McHenry during the War of 1812. The British launched rockets from boats in conjunction with artillery fire. During the rocket attack, Francis Scott Key, writing the words to the "Star-Spangled Banner," described the red glare of the rockets. Some forty years later, military rockets began to disappear as weapons, because artillery cannons became more efficient.

The first man to attempt to fly a rocket ship was a Chinese mandarin, Wanhu. About A.D. 1500, he had a bamboo chair "rocket ship" to which forty-seven of the largest rockets available were attached. He sat in the chair and held a large kite in each hand. The kites were to help him glide gently back to earth. At a signal, his assistants ignited the rockets. It is reported that there was a great roar, a blast of flame and smoke — and Wanhu and his ship disappeared. It is unlikely that he flew into space.

Who were the rocket pioneers? Although rockets disappeared as military weapons shortly after the Mexican War in 1847, they continued to be used for signaling at sea during distress, as flares to light battlefields and as fireworks. But the dream of space continued.

An American physicist, Dr. Robert Goddard, began to experiment with rockets in 1908. In 1919, when he published his first report, he revolutionized rocket theory. Up to that time, scientists believed that a rocket flew because its explosion pushed against the air. Dr. Goddard noted that rockets could fly even in "thin" air similar to that found

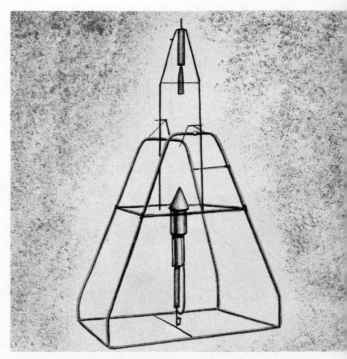

Goddard's first liquid fuel rocket was fired in 1926.

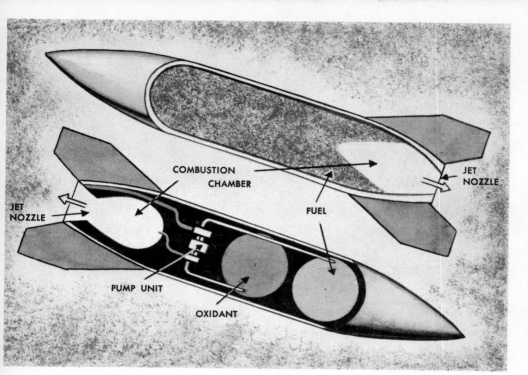

COMBUSTION CHAMBER

JET NOZZLE

FUEL

JET NOZZLE

PUMP UNIT

OXIDANT

The solid fuel rocket (top) is used for short-range guided missiles and as assisting devices for quick take-off of conventional and jet aircraft. The liquid fuel rocket (below) is used for long-range flights and when high speeds are needed, as in launching satellites.

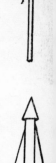

thousands of feet above the earth. He believed that rockets could be flown to the moon.

Although people ridiculed him and his work, Dr. Goddard continued to experiment. In 1926, he tested the first liquid fuel rocket. It traveled at 60 miles per hour and reached 184 feet in the air. His report and work inspired others in the field of rocketry. In 1929, in Germany, a rocket-propelled glider carried a man in flight.

In 1935, Dr. Goddard launched a gyroscope-controlled rocket. It rose almost 8,000 feet into the air and attained a speed of almost 700 miles per hour. About the same time, a group of Germans interested in rockets formed the *Verein für Raumschiffahrt,* the Rocket Society. One of its members was Count Wernher von Braun who, during World War II, directed rocket research at the German Research Facility at Peenemunde. After the war, von Braun came to the United States and has played a vital role in its rocket program.

What makes a rocket fly?

The basic rocket engine is the simplest of all power units for flight. It contains a combustion chamber and an exhaust nozzle. It needs no moving parts. The explosion of the propellent (explosive charge or fuel) escaping from the exhaust creates the forward thrust.

There are many different types of rockets, but they are classified into two groups — solid propellent and liquid propellent. The first group, solid propellents, are somewhat like the large firecrackers used on the Fourth of July. These rockets are powered by an explosive in powder or solid form. The final stage of the rocket that launched the first U. S. *Explorer Satellite* was a solid propellent rocket.

The liquid propellent rockets have more complex power units. It is necessary to have tanks within the rockets to hold the liquid and often pumps to control the flow of the liquid to the combustion chamber. The most commonly

43

used liquid fuel is alcohol and liquid oxygen, or *lox,* as it is often called. The lox, when pumped into a rocket just before blast-off, is extremely cold. Its temperature is −305°F.

Rockets differ from jets in that they are not airbreathing. Because the rockets carry their own oxygen to aid combustion, they can work even in a vacuum, where there is no air. There is no limit to the height they can reach.

Any unmanned rocket or ship, whose
What is a guided missile?
flight path can be altered while it is still in flight, is known as a guided missile. The first attempt at guided missiles was made by the Germans during World War II. They used V-1 rockets, actually pulsejet engines with explosives, to bombard London. These missiles flew at 360 miles per hour and had a range of about 125 miles. The German V-2 rockets were larger and more powerful. Their range was about 200 miles and they reached speeds of 3,000 miles per hour.

One system of classifying guided missiles is based on (a) where they are fired, and (b) the location of their target. For example, *surface-to-surface* missiles are fired from the ground to hit a target on the ground. Examples of surface-to-surface missiles are the Air Force *Atlas* and *Titan*. Both have a range of 8,000 to 8,500 miles and travel at a speed of over Mach 20 — twenty times the speed of sound. The Navy's *Polaris* is a surface-to-surface missile that can be fired from under water.

Surface-to-air missiles include the Navy's *Talos* and the Army's *Hercules*,

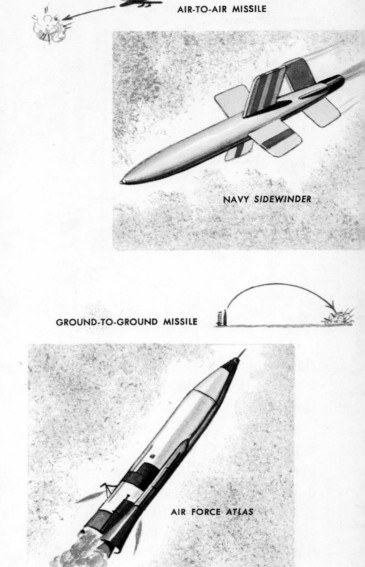

AIR-TO-AIR MISSILE

NAVY *SIDEWINDER*

GROUND-TO-GROUND MISSILE

AIR FORCE *ATLAS*

which travel at speeds of over Mach 3 and Mach 4. The Navy's *Sidewinder,* which exceeds a Mach 2.5 speed, is an *air-to-air* missile, while the Army's *Rascal* is an *air-to-surface* missile.

Guided missiles are controlled in flight
How do they guide missiles?
by radio, radar and electronic computers. When one radar beam picks up the target, it feeds the information about height, direction and speed to a computer. The electronic computer makes all the calculations

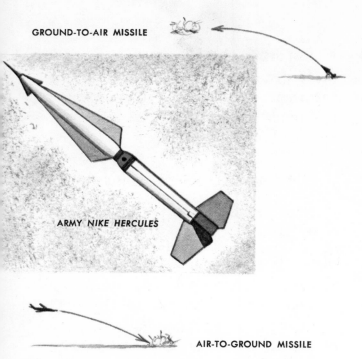

GROUND-TO-AIR MISSILE

ARMY NIKE HERCULES

AIR-TO-GROUND MISSILE

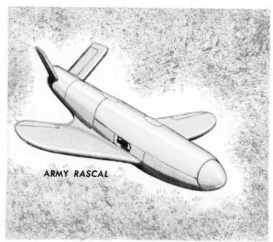

ARMY RASCAL

within seconds and it fires the missile. While in flight, the missile is "watched" by another radar beam, which tells the computer the missile's flight. The computer makes any changes in the missile's path by radio waves which control adjustment motors within the missile, until it hits the target.

A similar radar, radio and electronic computer system is used to launch and guide rockets as they go off into space. Large radar and radio telescope units "follow" the rocket as it plunges into space. If the rocket veers off course, these watchers inform the computer and it radios the rocket, making the necessary changes to correct its course.

Why does a satellite stay up in the sky? You know that if you throw a ball into the air, it will fall back to earth. This "pull" of the earth is called *gravity*. There is a rule which governs moving bodies — a moving body will continue to travel in a straight line unless acted on by another force.

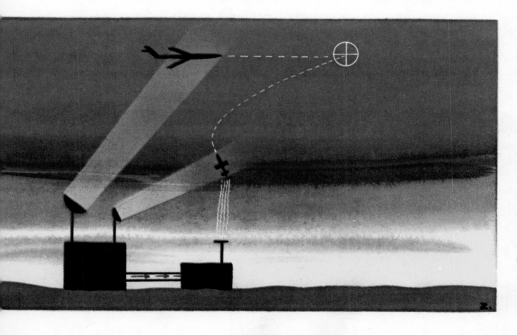

The main radar scanner (left) picks up approaching aircraft. A computer works out the plane's speed, path, height, weather conditions and other factors. The ground missile is automatically made ready and fired by the computer. A smaller radar guides the missile through the air until it reaches the enemy target.

If the ball were shot up like a rocket, traveling at about 18,000 miles per hour, to a height of 300 miles, it would be affected by two forces. One is the force of gravity that would pull it back to earth, and the other is the force that would tend to keep it moving in a straight line. At this speed and at this height, these two forces would be about equal. As a result, the ball would continue to spin around the earth. That is just what the satellite does.

The speed needed to overcome the earth's gravitational pull is called the *escape velocity*. You can compare this with rolling a toy automobile up a small hill. If the car is not pushed fast enough, it will slow up as it goes up the hill, stop for an instant and then roll back down the hill. If it is pushed fast enough, it will roll over the top of the hill and continue rolling. That escape velocity from the earth is about 25,000 miles per hour. Thus, for a satellite to remain in orbit,

it must attain a speed of at least 18,000 miles per hour. If it is to escape the earth's gravitational pull in order to go into outer space, it must be traveling at over 25,000 miles per hour.

Satellites have been used to discover the mysteries of the upper atmosphere and interplanetary space. Satellites with various shapes have been used, including spheres, cones, cylinders, spheres with paddles and even a giant balloon. Each of the satellites has been packed with scientific instruments, and their readings have been sent back to earth by radio. We have even mounted photographic and television cameras in satellites.

What do satellites see and *tell*?

While the initial satellites tested our ability to put a satellite into orbit and to track it, the later ones went into space on specific probes. *Explorer I* studied the cosmic rays, or van Allen radiation belt, around the earth. *Vanguard I* measured the density of the air in our upper atmosphere and space.

The Russian *Lunik* satellites were moon "explorers." *Lunik I* studied the atmosphere around the moon, *Lunik II*

CENTRIFUGAL FORCE

ORBIT

GRAVITY

Rockets carry satellite into the air so it can take off under its own power. The satellite is kept in orbit as the centrifugal force is balanced by the gravitational pull of the earth.

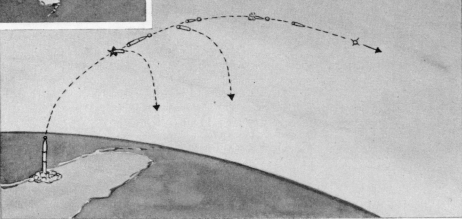

landed on the moon, and *Lunik III* photographed the "dark side" of the moon, the side which no man had ever seen before.

The American *Tiros I,* equipped with television cameras and transmitters, sent back TV pictures of the cloud covers over the earth. *Explorer XII* tested our ability to recover a capsule returned to earth from the satellite. *Echo I* was put into orbit to aid long-range voice communications by bouncing radio-wave telephone messages off its massive surface.

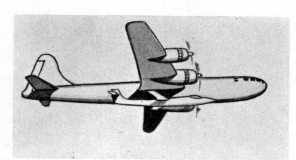

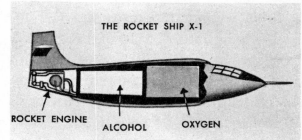

THE ROCKET SHIP X-1

ROCKET ENGINE   ALCOHOL   OXYGEN

Steppingstones Into Space

On October 14, 1947, there were two

Has man flown in a rocket?

planes some six miles up in the sky over California. One was a four-engine B-29 and the other, painted bright orange, was fastened to the B-29's underside. Suddenly, the orange plane, like a stone fired from a slingshot, soared upward and exceeded Mach 1, the speed of sound. That plane was the X-1, a rocket ship piloted by Captain Charles E. Yeager.

The X-1 was shaped like a .50-caliber bullet. It was 31 feet long and its wingspan was 28 feet. It was powered by a rocket engine using liquid oxygen and alcohol as fuel.

Some six years later, Yeager flew the X-1A. He zoomed more than 90,000 feet into the air, traveling at a speed of 1,650 miles per hour. These early rocket ships were followed by others, including the X-3, the *Flying Stiletto,* and the X-5, the *Flying Guppy.*

The X-15, an outstanding rocket ship, was developed for speeds of up to 4,000 miles per hour and a flight ceiling of 100 miles. This 50-foot ship has a 22-foot wingspan and is launched in the air from a giant B-52 at 40,000 to 50,000 feet. Its rocket engine is designed to fire for only 90 seconds. After that the rocket glides back to earth. Many consider the X-15 the first true manned rocket ship.

On October 11, 1961, Major Robert M. White set an altitude record in the X-15 by flying it more than 41 miles above the earth. On November 9, 1961, in a maximum effort, he set a speed record of 4,070 miles per hour.

The X-15 is the forerunner of the first real space rocket, the Boeing *Dyna-Soar.* This manned rocket is designed for speeds of up to Mach 25 — twenty-five times the speed of sound, or 17,000 miles per hour. It is designed so that it can escape the earth's atmosphere.

On April 27, 1959, seven astronauts (AS-tro-nauts) — three from the Air Force, three from the Navy and one from the Marine Corps — were selected for *Project Mercury*.

What is Project Mercury?

This project has three objectives: (1) to study man's ability to travel in space; (2) to place a manned satellite in orbit around the earth; and (3) to return the pilot safely to earth.

A special capsule has been built to hold the pilot. This cone-shaped capsule, 7 feet in diameter at its base and 10 feet long, will be the satellite which is eventually placed in orbit by a rocket. Within the capsule, the pilot will be strapped to a couchlike frame to support him against the intense pressures during take-off and landing. The cone-capsule will go into orbit at 100 to 150 miles above the earth. At re-entry time, retro-rockets, attached to the capsule, will be fired. This will slow the capsule and make it return to earth. The capsule has a special re-entry shield to protect the pilot from the intense heat that will be created when the capsule re-enters the earth's atmosphere.

On April 12, 1961, the Soviet Union launched the first manned satellite to orbit the earth. The 5-ton space vehicle

Space craft will one day land on the earth's moon.

reached a 188-mile height and, traveling at a speed exceeding 17,000 miles per hour, circled the earth in 89.1 minutes. The Russian pilot, Major Yuri Gagarin, was returned to earth alive.

On May 5, 1961, the United States launched its first manned satellite. It was also the world's first space flight controlled by a pilot — Navy Commander Alan B. Shepard Jr. The 2,000-pound Mercury capsule, named *Freedom 7,* was fired by a Redstone rocket. The craft, traveling at a speed of 4,500 miles per hour, reached an altitude of 115 miles during the 15-minute trip.

Man no longer needs to envy the bird.

What about the future?

Not only can he fly faster and farther than any bird, but he can also fly in the air-thin atmosphere.

Man has always been curious about space — the moon, planets, other worlds. As far back as A.D. 160, the Greek philosopher, Lucian of Samosata, wrote a tale about a trip to the moon. Today, man is at the threshold of space, ready to turn fictional moon journeys into reality.

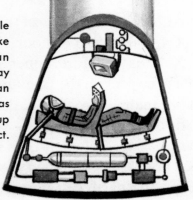

The Mercury capsule was designed to take the first American into space. On May 5, 1961, Com. Alan B. Shepard Jr. was fired 115 miles up in the U. S. project.

THE HOW AND WHY WONDER BOOK OF
SOUND

Written by
MARTIN L. KEEN

Illustrated by
GEORGE J. ZAFFO

Editorial Production:
DONALD D. WOLF

Edited under the supervision of
Dr. Paul E. Blackwood
Washington, D. C.

Text and illustrations approved by
Oakes A. White, Brooklyn Children's Museum, Brooklyn, New York

GROSSET & DUNLAP • **Publishers** • **NEW YORK**

Introduction

The study of sound will lead to one interesting thing after another, as you will quickly discover in this book. What is sound? Why do sounds differ? Why are sounds loud and soft, pleasant or unpleasant, musical or noisy? *The How and Why Wonder Book of Sound* answers these and dozens of other basic questions on this subject.

But perhaps even more interesting than the characteristics of sound are its uses. For example, housekeepers will be pleased to discover that dishes can be washed with sound. There are also ways of recording your heartbeats for careful study by the doctor. As you will read, knowledge of sound has always been put to good use in dozens of ways. Talking and music are but two everyday examples. But with the astonishing development of electricity and electronics, the study of sound has become an even more important science. *Sonar* and *stereophonic* are but two key words that suggest the modern uses of this branch of study.

You will find numerous experiments in *The How and Why Wonder Book of Sound*. They illustrate the basic ideas about sound and they are fun to do. While experimenting, inquiring, investigating and exploring to answer questions about the subject, you will cultivate the very skills needed to become a scientist.

Children, as well as parents and teachers, will find this book a valuable source of information.

Paul E. Blackwood

Dr. Blackwood is a professional employee in the U. S. Office of Education. This book was edited by him in his private capacity and no official support or endorsement by the Office of Education is intended or should be inferred.

Library of Congress Catalog Card Number: 62-9675

Contents

RADIO AND TV STORE

Look at the illustration and try to imagine the world without sound.

Turn off the sound on your TV set and you can better understand what a world without sound would be like.

Sometimes it would be a blessing if there were no sound.

A World Without Sound

We are always surrounded by a sea of sound. There is not a minute of the day when we cannot hear some sound. To get an idea of how big a part sound plays in our lives, imagine what the world would be like without sound. Imagine yourself on a busy street where traffic moves silently. Automobile engines run soundlessly, there is no screech of brakes and an automobile horn never toots. People walk with silent footsteps and close doors noiselessly. Someone drops a few coins which strike the pavement, bounce and roll without the familiar jingling sound. Some work-

5

men unloading a truck drop a crate. It strikes the street and breaks open as noiselessly as if it were only the shadow of a crate. A man whistles to his dog, but the animal still runs about, because no shrill sounds leave his master's lips. You see a friend and call to him, but he continues on his way, because no shout leaps from your mouth.

Many sounds give us pleasure. Almost everyone enjoys music and singing. Think how mournful the world would be if you could not listen to music, nor sing nor whistle when you are happy. On a quiet summer afternoon, the songs of birds, the hum of insects, the rustle of the breeze in the leaves, and perhaps the soft murmur of a brook — all these things give us pleasure, but none of them would exist in a soundless world.

Our safety depends to a large degree on sound. The baby's cry brings his mother quickly to his aid. Everybody recognizes the cry, "Help!" as a signal that someone is in danger. At traffic crossings, the shriek of a train whistle or the blast of an automobile horn warn of approaching danger. Ships in a fog warn of their presence by the croaking of foghorns. In a forest, the cracking sound of a tree about to fall warns the lumberjack to jump out of the way of danger. How difficult it would be to avoid danger in a world without sound.

The most common way mankind communicates thoughts is by talking; that is, by making the sounds we call words. Think how different our lives would be if we could not talk. We could, of course, still communicate with one another by signs, as deaf persons do. But then we would always have to look directly at the person talking to us. We could never talk to someone in the next room nor call to a friend we see on the street. Communicating with large groups would be difficult. A speaker, instead of using a microphone, would probably have his magnified image projected on a large screen, so that the audience could see his hand- and finger-signs. Instead of the telephone for long distance communication, we would probably have some system of blinking colored lights to spell out words in a code. No one would have invented radio, and the first type of broadcasting might have been television — silent television.

Without sound, then, our world would lose some of its beauty. It would be a more dangerous place, and one in which communication would be difficult and cumbersome.

Without sound, we all might have to make use of smoke signals.

The Nature of Sound

What is sound?

Sound is a form of energy that is produced by a vibrating object. (Energy is the capacity or ability to do work — to move something — to give it a push or pull.) To vibrate means to move back and forth. The hum given out by a plucked rubber band is due to the

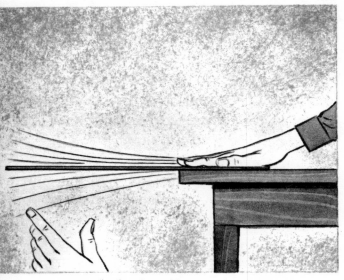

A vibrating object produces sound.

back-and-forth motions of the rubber band. You can easily see the band vibrate; it looks blurry as it moves to and fro. If you strike a fork edgewise on a table, you can see the prongs vibrate at the same time you hear the musical note they give forth. As the prongs vibrate less, the sound dies away.

Firmly hold a ruler, or some other wooden lathe or a nail file on a table so that about two-thirds of the ruler projects over the edge of the table. Then pull downward on the free end of the ruler and suddenly let go. You will see the ruler vibrate up and down at the same time you hear a humming sound.

How can you prove that sound is a form of energy?

Obtain a cardboard tube about an inch-and-a-half in diameter. A mailing tube will do very well. If you can't get a mailing tube, roll a sheet of thick paper, about a foot wide, into a tube and fasten it with adhesive tape. Roll a small piece of paper into the shape of a cone and fasten it, too, with adhesive tape. The base of this cone should not be much wider than the diameter of the tube. Fasten the cone to one end of the tube by means of adhesive tape. Now, cut off the tip of the cone, so that you leave a hole a little more than one-fourth of an inch wide.

Cover the other end of the tube with a thin piece of rubber, such as that from a toy balloon. The rubber should be stretched tightly over the end of the tube. Affix the rubber in place with adhesive tape.

Place a lighted candle on a table.

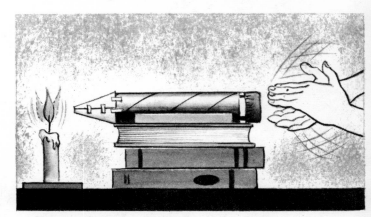

The sound waves will blow out the candle.

Using books, prop the tube in such a position that the hole in the cone points directly at the candle flame. It should

7

also be no more than half an inch from the flame. Be careful not to set the paper on fire!

Now, clap your hands together sharply just behind the tube. The candle flame will suddenly wave about. What moved the flame? Since passage of air through the tube was blocked by the rubber, the flame was not moved simply by wind from your hands moving through the tube. Some form of energy had to pass through the tube to move the flame. This energy was provided by the sound of your hand-clapping.

You may wonder how you can hear the back-and-forth movements of a vibrating object. After all, the vibrating object does not touch your ears. You can hear the vibrations because the air conducts the vibrations to your ears.

How do we hear sounds that are far away?

In its role as a carrier of vibrations between the object and your ears, the air is known as a *medium*. This term comes from the Latin word *medius,* which means "middle." Air serves as a middle, or go-between, to bring the vibrations from the object to your ears.

Air is not the only medium that will conduct sound; other gases will do the same. Liquids and solids are even better conductors of sound. Place a watch on a bare wooden table and press your ear to the other end of the table. You will clearly hear the ticking of the watch. The next time you go swimming, get two stones, put your head under the water and bang the stones together. You will be surprised at how loud a sound the stones make. Ask a friend to stand in the water about 150 feet from you. Let him bang the stones together in the air. Listen to the sound it makes. Then, after you have ducked your head beneath the surface, let your friend bang the stones together in the water. The underwater bang will be much louder, proving that water is a better sound-conducting medium than air.

The watch on the table proved that solids are good conductors of sound. Here is another way you can prove the same thing: With a small nail, punch a hole in the center of the bottom of each of two tin cans. Thread a long, stout string through the holes. Tie a thick knot at each end of the string so that it cannot be pulled through the hole.

Ask a friend to take one can and walk away from you — far enough to stretch the string tight. Place the can over your ear. If your friend now speaks in a low

The string in a tin-can telephone has to be kept taut and should not touch anything.

top of a domed glass container called a bell jar. We place the bell jar on a circular metal plate upon which there is a thin layer of grease. The grease is used to make an airtight seal around the bottom of the bell jar. In the center of the circular metal plate is a hole that leads — through a rubber hose — to a vacuum pump.

THE CHIMES OF CUTLERY

To the middle portion of a three-foot piece of string, tie a knife, a fork and a spoon about one inch apart. With your fingertips, hold an end of the string in each ear. Let the pieces of silverware swing freely so that they collide with each other. The string will conduct chime-like sounds to your ears. Remove the ends of the string from your ears and note how different the jangling cutlery sounds when air is the conducting medium.

voice into the can at his end, you will hear him clearly. Ask him to remove the can from his mouth and to speak again in the same low voice.

Since you can barely — if at all — hear your friend's voice, then it was the string that conducted the sound of his voice to your ear.

We have just learned that sound travels

How can we prove that sound needs a medium to travel through?

through a medium — solid, liquid or gaseous. How can we prove that the medium is necessary — that sound would not travel if there were no medium? We tape a pair of small, powerful electric dry-cell batteries to the back of a door bell. Then we connect the batteries to the bell, so that the bell rings.

With a strong thread, we suspend the bell and batteries upside down from the

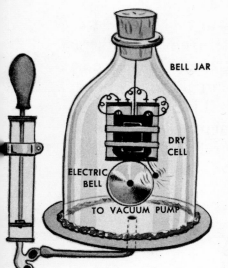

With the experiment described and illustrated below, you can demonstrate the principle that as a vacuum is created, it causes sound to fade. Another experiment might be easier. With a pin and thread, suspend a small bell (or a couple of pieces of metal that can jangle) from the bottom of a cork that tightly fits the mouth of a flask. Heat water in the flask. When the water boils, turn off the heat, and immediately place the cork securely in the mouth of the flask. (Be careful! The neck of the flask will be hot.) When the flask has cooled, shake it, and note how faintly the bell sounds. Steam drove some air from the flask to create a partial vacuum.

We start the pump, which begins to take air out of the bell jar. At first we clearly hear the bell continuing to ring inside the jar. Soon, however, the sound of the bell becomes fainter. As more and more air is removed from the bell jar, the sound continues to become fainter and fainter, until we can no longer hear the bell at all.

What happened to the sound? We can still see the bell ringing, so we know that nothing has happened to the source of the sound. Evidently, something is now missing that formerly conducted the sound of the bell to our ears. Since the air pumped from the bell jar is the only missing item, we can safely conclude it was this air that had conducted the sound of the bell.

If we now let air slowly return through the hose to the bell jar, the ringing reappears and gradually grows louder.

SOUND WAVES

What do we mean by compression waves? Sound travels through a medium in the form of waves. Let us take sound traveling through air as an example. When a vibrating object, say the prong of a tuning fork, moves in one direction, it pushes the air in front of it. This crowded section of air pushes against the air next to itself, a little farther out from the vibrating prong. The crowding motion that moves farther and farther out from the vibrating object is called a *compression wave*.

What do we mean by rarefaction waves? While the vibrating prong of a tuning fork compresses the air on one side of itself, it pulls away from the air on the other side and leaves an empty space. The adjacent air begins to rush into this empty space. The place of this inrushing air is taken by the air a little farther out, which, in turn, leaves an empty space behind itself. And the empty space moves outward from the moving prong in the same manner as the compression wave. Although we have said that the space behind the moving prong is empty, actually, it is not entirely without air. Rather, the air in this space is much thinner, or rarer, than air normally is. This zone of rarefied air, moving farther and farther out from a vibrating object, is called a *rarefaction wave*.

So far, we have told only half the story.

What do we mean by longitudinal waves?

We have seen what happens when the prong of a tuning fork moves in one direction. But a vibrating object moves back and forth. So we must now see what happens when the prong moves in the direction opposite from the one we have been describing. When the prong moves in the opposite direction, it produces a new compression wave in the direction it is moving, and a new rarefaction wave behind itself.

One compression and the following rarefaction (or one rarefaction and the following compression), together, comprise one *sound wave*. Waves of this kind are called *longitudinal* waves. They move outward from a vibrating object like a series of expanding soap bubbles. The bubbles themselves represent the compression waves, and the

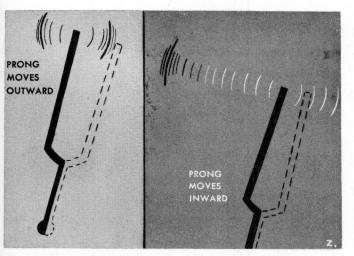

The diagrams illustrate the effect produced by one prong of a vibrating tuning fork. As the prong moves outward, a compression wave starts; as it moves inward, a rarefaction wave starts.

spaces between the bubbles represent the rarefaction waves.

If an object vibrates less than sixteen times a second, it does not produce sound waves, because air particles slip around it, instead of being compressed into waves.

To make some of these facts a little easier to visualize, just imagine

Compression wave: How does it work?

a long train of railroad cars standing on a track. An engine backs against a car at one end of

From a vibrating tuning fork or any other vibrating object, sound waves spread in every direction, each consisting of one compression and one rarefaction.

the train. This pushes the car against the one behind it. The second car pushes against the third, the third against the fourth, and so on. The push imparted by the engine passes along the whole line of cars in much the same way as a compression wave passes through the air — or any other type of sound-conform the compression wave; rather, it is energy in the form of an impulse that is transmitted from one section of air to the next.

Now think again of the railroad train we used as an example of compression.

Rarefaction wave: How does it work?

You remember that the engine backed into the line of cars and sent a compression impulse along the whole train. Having attached itself to the train, the engine now moves forward. The coupling devices that hold the cars together are slightly elastic — they have some give in them — so that the whole train does not immediately move forward as a unit behind the engine's first forward pull. Instead, the first car moves forward, leaving a little wider space between itself and the second car. The elastic coupling device then pulls the second car forward, and the original distance between the first two cars is restored. Now, however, the distance between the second and third cars has widened momentarily. This momentary widening passes all along the whole

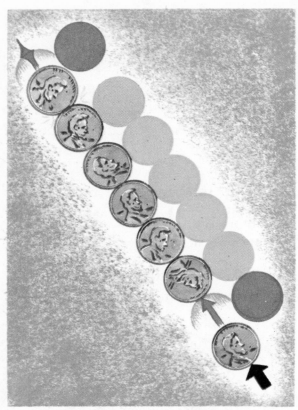

THE COIN THAT GOT AWAY!

On a smooth table, put six coins touching one another in a straight line. Place another coin half an inch directly behind the line. With a flip of your finger, cause this coin to strike the rear of the line. You will see the front coin move forward away from the line. The coin you flip transfers its energy of motion to the line of coins. This energy moves along the line in the form of an impulse that pushes the first coin away from the line.

ducting medium. It is important to note that it is not a railroad car that passes from one end of the line to the other, but rather energy in the form of an impulse. An impulse is a force that starts an object moving. So, the push of the engine is an impulse. Keeping this in mind, you can see that it is not the air next to a vibrating object that moves outward to

The railroad engine, starting to pull the train forward, transmits impulses through the coupling devices. This affects all the other cars in much the same way that a vibrating object produces a rarefaction wave.

length of the cars, in much the same way that a rarefaction wave moves through air or some other sound-conducting medium.

Now that we know what sound waves are, we can better understand why the sound of the bell in the bell jar faded away and finally stopped. As the air was pumped from inside the bell jar, there was less and less of a medium in which the vibrating bell could produce compression and rarefaction waves. At last, the air became so thin that the bell could not produce sound waves at all, and we could no longer hear the bell.

Let us take a tuning fork and clamp it firmly to an upright support, so that the prongs are horizontal.

How can we make a vibration write its autograph?

Next, we affix, with sealing wax or some other adhesive, a thin wire or bristle of a brush to the upper surface of one prong, so that the wire projects outward and downward from the end of the prong. We hold a small pane of window glass over a candle flame until the lower surface of the glass is covered by soot.

When the smoked glass has cooled, we place it on some books — the sooty side up. We arrange the height of the books so that the tip of the wire rests lightly on the sooty surface, near one end of the glass. We draw the books along the table straight toward ourselves, so that the end of the wire traces a line in the soot. If we have carefully pulled the books in a straight line, then the line traced by the wire will be straight, too.

Carefully lifting the tip of the wire just a fraction of an inch off the glass, we push the books back to their original position. We release the tip of the wire, and it is now resting on the beginning of the line we have traced. Now, we strike the tuning fork a horizontal blow with a pencil, and again pull the books straight toward us. This time, the tip of the wire traces a wavy line in the soot.

Let us study the lines we have traced. The straight line represents a tuning-fork prong that is not moving. It also represents the point from which a vibrating prong begins its movement in one direction, and to which the moving prong returns before beginning to move in the

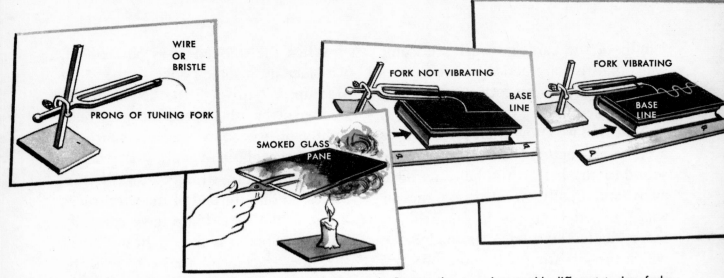

A vibrating prong of a tuning fork writes its autograph. Repeat the experiment with different tuning forks.

opposite direction. As the curved line moves outward from the straight center line, the curve represents a compression. As the curve moves back past the center line, the curve represents a rarefaction. Thus, the wavy line is the autograph of a vibrating tuning-fork prong, and *also* the autograph of a sound wave.

Measuring Sound

One way to measure the speed at which sound travels through air is quite simple. Exactly one mile from a group of measuring instruments, a small explosive charge is set off. The light from the explosion travels the intervening mile in 1/186,000 of a second — a time so short that we can ignore it and say that at the same instant the explosion takes place, the flash is recorded by an instrument a mile away. Shortly, another instrument records the sound of the explosion; that is, it records the arrival of the first sound wave from the explosion. The time interval between the recordings of the flash and

How fast does sound travel?

the sound is the time it takes the sound to travel one mile through air. We find the time to be five seconds. Then in one second, the sound travels one-fifth of a mile.

Scientists have made many measurements of the speed of sound. They have learned that sound travels faster in a warm medium than in a cool medium. For example, at freezing temperature — 32° Fahrenheit — sound travels through air at 1,088 feet per second. At room temperature — 68° F. — the speed of sound through air is 1,129 feet per second. And at 1,800° F., the speed rises to 2,300 feet per second.

Measurements have shown that

sound travels through liquids faster than through air or other gases — and through solids faster than through liquids. For example, sound waves travel through water at room temperature almost 5,000 feet per second — nearly five times as fast as through air. In an iron bar at the same temperature, the speed of sound is more than 16,000 feet per second — fourteen times as fast as through air.

We just learned how the flash and sound of an explosion can be used to measure the speed of sound.

How can you use sound to measure distance?

Now you will learn how you can use a flash of light and accompanying sound to measure distance. We cannot give you an explosive to provide the light and sound, but if you are patient, nature will provide you with these two things, free. All you have to do is to wait for a thunderstorm. The lightning flash and the accompanying thunder are just what you need.

However, before using lightning and thunder to measure distance, let us spend a moment to learn what thunder and lightning are. A bolt of lightning is a giant electric spark leaping between a cloud and the earth, or between two clouds. This huge spark not only sends out a great flash of light, but also a large amount of heat. This heat expands the air surrounding the spark so violently that the air is given a sharp push. As a result, a powerful sound wave travels outward from the zone of heated air. When this wave reaches you, you hear it as a clap of thunder. When lightning flashes nearby, you can clearly detect the powerful sound wave as a single deafening thunderclap. When the lightning is farther away, the sound wave may bounce from cloud to cloud, or from clouds to hills, before it reaches you. As a result of the bouncing, you hear the thunder, not as a single loud clap, but as a series of deep-toned rolling sounds.

The light from a lightning flash reaches you practically instantly, but you have to wait for the sound of the thunder. If you count the seconds between the lightning flash and the first

How can you tell the distance of a lightning flash?

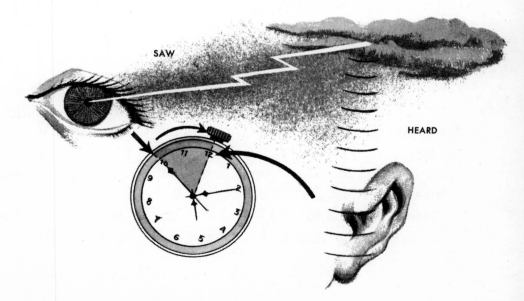

Count the seconds between a lightning flash and the sound of thunder. Then divide this number by five. The answer will tell you how many miles away the lightning struck.

SAW

HEARD

sound of the thunder, and then divide the number of seconds by five, the result will be the approximate distance in miles of the lightning flash. Why? Because at thunderstorm temperature, sound travels in air about one-fifth of a mile a second. If ten seconds elapse between the time you see lightning flash and hear thunder, the lightning is two miles away: 10 divided by 5 equals 2.

When we speak about the "high" or "low" of a sound, we

What is the pitch of a sound?

are talking about its *pitch*. A piccolo has a higher pitch than a tuba. The pitch of a canary's chirp is higher than the mooing of a cow. The keys on the right-hand side of a piano have a higher pitch than the keys on the left-hand side.

What is responsible for differences in pitch? Pitch depends on the number of vibrations per second made by a sound-producing object. The number of vibrations per second is called the *frequency* of the sound. The higher the frequency, the higher the pitch.

Scientists speak of frequency in terms of *cycles*. For instance, middle C of a piano is a sound that vibrates 256 times a second, so we say that the frequency of middle C is 256 cycles per second.

We learned that vibrations may be represented by a wavy line, such as we traced on smoked glass. As we were tracing the wavy line, time was passing. Only a certain number of wavy lines were traced in each second. If we had measured how far we moved the smoked glass in one second, and if we had made a mark on the straight line at the end of each second, we then could have counted the number of wavy lines between each mark. This count would have given us the number of vibrations per second — the *frequency* — of the tuning fork.

Let us make a mark on any part of the wavy line that represents a vibration. Then, we make a mark on the same part of the next wavy line, and so on. The distance between the two marks — as measured on the straight line — is called the *wave length* of the vibration.

If you think about what you have just learned, you will see that the shorter the wave length, the greater the number of vibrations that can take place in a second. In other words, the shorter the wave length, the higher the frequency. Since we know that high frequency results in high pitch, we can now say that short wave length also results in high pitch. We can now also say that notes from a piccolo not only have a high pitch, but also high frequency and short wave length. Notes from a tuba have low pitch, low frequency and long wave length.

Musicians say that persons who can distinguish

What do musicians mean by "tone deaf"?

readily between different pitch have a "good ear," while those who have difficulty in distinguishing pitch have a "poor ear." It is possible to acquire a "good ear" by practice, although for some persons learning this is very difficult. Some persons cannot learn to distinguish different pitches at all and are said to be "tone deaf."

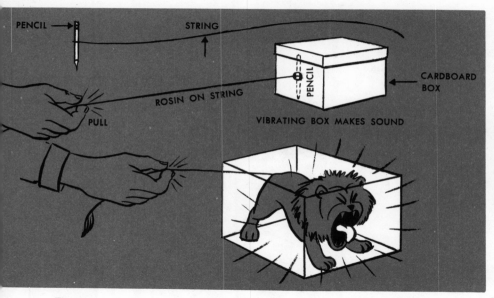

PENCIL → STRING

ROSIN ON STRING

PULL

PENCIL

CARDBOARD BOX

VIBRATING BOX MAKES SOUND

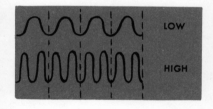

LOW

HIGH

Tie one end of a string about two feet long around the middle of a short pencil. Cut a hole about half an inch across in the center of one side of a cardboard or wooden box. Put the string through the hole so that the pencil is inside the box. Hold the box with one hand. Grip the string between the thumb and forefinger of the other hand, and pull outward, so that the string slips with difficulty through your fingers. From the box will come a lion's roar, a chicken's squawk or a dog's bark, depending on the size of the box and how the string slips through your fingers. The sounds will be greatly increased if you rub plenty of rosin on the string. If you can't get rosin, chalk dust will do. Your fingers slipping along the string cause vibrations that the string transmits to the box, which, in turn, vibrates and magnifies the sound.

Use a compass to draw a circle at least six inches in diameter on a piece of cardboard. Draw another circle with the same center but with a diameter three inches smaller than the first. The inner circle will then have its circumference an inch-and-a-half from that of the larger circle. Cut the larger circle out of the cardboard. Now, cut triangular notches that reach from the outer edge of the circle to the inner circle. This will produce one-and-a-half-inch teeth all around the inner circle.

How can you prove that pitch depends on frequency?

Obtain a hexagonal — six-sided — pencil, sharpened at both ends. Slowly push a point of the pencil through the center of the cardboard disk, until about half the pencil projects on each side.

Make a stand from fairly thick wire. A coat hanger will provide the needed wire. You will probably need a pair of pliers to bend the wire properly.

Place the pencil and cardboard disk on the stand, as shown. Obtain a drinking straw or some other thin tube. Spin the disk with one hand, while blowing air from the straw at the teeth on the disk. (It may be easier to work this experiment with the help of a friend. One of you can turn the disk and the other can direct the stream of air.)

You will note that when the disk is turning fast, the pitch of the sound made by the air striking the disk's teeth will be high. When the disk is turning slower, the pitch will be lower. The stream of air striking one of the moving teeth on the rim of the disk, and then moving past the tooth as the disk turns, causes the air to vibrate fast enough to produce sound waves. The frequency of these vibrations depends on the number

PENCIL WITH CARD WHEEL

Pitch depends on frequency. When the disk turns rapidly, sound will be higher than when it turns slowly.

of teeth passing in front of the straw. The faster the disk spins, the more teeth pass in front of the straw, and the higher is the pitch of the sound.

Although this experiment clearly shows

How do the scientists give proof that pitch depends on frequency?

that pitch depends on frequency, you will find that the range of pitch is very limited. For this reason, let us see how scientists perform the same experiment with precision equipment. They use a siren — a metal disk with evenly-spaced holes punched in a circle near the disk's rim. A nozzle is fixed so that air passing through it strikes the disk at the point where the holes pass when the disk is turned. Puffs of air passing through the holes give rise to a sound, the frequency

of which is determined by the number of puffs per second. And, of course, the number of puffs per second is determined by the speed at which the disk turns. The frequency of a sound made by a siren can be calculated very easily, if one knows how many turns per second the disk is making. The frequency is equal to the number of turns per second multiplied by the number of holes. For example, if a siren's disk has 36 holes and turns 100 times per second, the frequency of the sound is 3,600 cycles per second.

You may be able to sing a note that has

What is loudness?

exactly the same pitch as a locomotive whistle or a factory whistle, but you surely cannot sing as loud. What determines the loudness of a sound? Loudness depends on the amount of energy that goes into making a sound. You know that it is easier to whisper than to shout as loud as you can. When you shout, you put much more energy into making a sound than when you whisper.

If you drop a whole brick on a wooden floor, it will make a louder sound than if you drop only a small piece of the brick. The whole brick strikes the floor with more energy than the small piece. Perhaps you have been near a quarry when a dynamite blast was set off. You not only heard the blast as a loud sound, but you probably seemed to feel a physical blow at the same time. What you felt was a strong compression wave produced by the great energy of the explosion.

Let us examine loudness in terms of our curve tracing on smoked glass. If we have two tuning forks vibrating at the same pitch, they will trace the same number of curved lines in a second of time, because both have the same frequency. But if one tuning fork is louder than the other, how will its curve differ? Its curves will reach farther out from the center line on each side. This means that the prongs of the louder tuning fork move farther back and forth as they vibrate.

The distance the curve moves outward from the center line is called the *amplitude* of the vibration represented by the curve. So, then, louder sounds have waves with greater amplitudes than do softer sounds.

Now, when any object is moved, work is done. And it takes energy to do work. The more the work, the more the energy needed. Therefore, to move the prongs of the louder tuning fork farther requires more energy. Thus, more energy is needed for louder sound.

SIREN

To measure loudness, engineers have worked out a scale that **How is loudness measured?** depends on the amount of energy carried by sound waves. The unit of this loudness scale is the *bel,* named in honor of Alexander Graham Bell, inventor of the telephone. However, sound engineers have found it easier to work with a smaller unit, the *decibel,* which is one-tenth of a bel. Decibels are measured on an instrument, called a *sound-level meter,* that changes sound energy to electrical energy. The sound energy can then be read on the dial of an electric meter. On this meter, zero decibels represents a sound just a little fainter than the human ear can hear, and 100 decibels represent a sound ten billion times as loud.

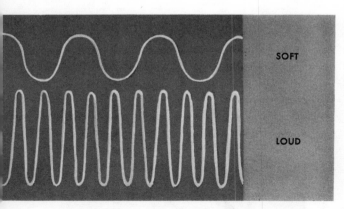

SOFT

LOUD

The higher the top of the wave from the base line on the pane, the louder is the sound. More energy is needed for the louder sound.

Following is a table of the loudness measurements of some familiar sounds:

SOUND	DECIBELS	DESCRIPTION
Thunder	120	Painfully loud
Airplane engine	100-120	Painfully loud
Pneumatic drill	90	Very loud
Heavy traffic	90	Very loud
Hi-fi record player	70	Loud
Ordinary conversation	40-50	Moderate
Quiet home	30	Faint
Whisper	10	Very faint
Rustling of leaves on a tree	10	Very faint

You know that a sound far away is fainter than the same sound nearby.

Why are farther sounds fainter?

The sound of an airplane becomes louder as it approaches overhead, and then fades as the plane flies farther away. So, the farther a sound travels, the fainter it becomes. We have learned enough about sound to understand why loudness fades as sound travels. We know that sound is energy in the form of an impulse that gives particles of air, or other material, a series of motions called waves. We also know that to move anything requires energy, and that energy is used up as the object is moved. The farther a sound wave travels, the more air particles in its path are moved. This means that energy is used up as the sound wave moves along, and the sound wave carries less and less energy. Less energy in a sound wave means less loudness. Thus, the farther a sound moves, the fainter it becomes.

Suppose we have two tuning forks of the same pitch. We strike one to set it vibrating.

What is resonance?

The other tuning fork will vibrate, too, even though it is several feet from the first fork. Now, let us repeat this experiment with two tuning forks that do not have the same pitch. What happens this time? The tuning fork we strike fails to cause the other fork to vibrate. Why? Because a tuning fork vibrates with only one frequency — the frequency of its pitch. Sound waves produced by one tuning fork strike the other fork. These sound waves will cause the fork they strike to vibrate only if it has the same pitch as the fork that produces the sound waves. When one object vibrates as a result of regular impulses sent out by another vibrating object, we say that the objects are in *resonance*.

Every object has its own particular

Thread a needle with a piece of thread a foot long. Tie the ends of the thread together. Stick the needle into a small piece of cork. Strike a tuning fork lightly, and place it upright on a table. Suspend the cork so that it just touches the vibrating prong. Note how far the prong moves the cork. Repeat this experiment, striking the tuning fork hard this time. Note how much farther the cork is moved now. When the tuning fork was struck harder, its prongs moved farther back and forth, but they did not move faster. The sound was louder and the waves were stronger.

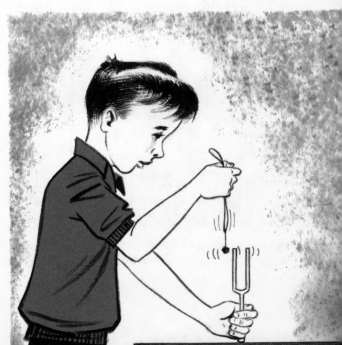

Obtain two empty soda bottles of the same size. Hold one so that its mouth is close to your ear. Ask a friend to stand a few feet from you and to blow strongly across the top of the other bottle until he produces a clear musical tone. When he does this, you will hear the same tone come from your bottle, though more faintly, of course. The vibrations of your friend's bottle caused resonant vibrations in your bottle.

frequency to which it vibrates. This frequency depends mainly on the object's size and shape and the material of which it is made. Perhaps you have been sitting in a quiet room and have heard a window pane suddenly buzz, or some object — maybe a sugar bowl lid or vase — unexpectedly rattle. These objects were vibrating in resonance with sound waves that may have been set in motion by a distant train or truck. The waves then traveled through the ground to your house.

If you have a piano available, you can easily demonstrate how resonance acts. Place a pin, a coin, a pencil or any other small, hard object on the music rack. Beginning at one end of the piano, strike the keys in order. As you pick your way along the keyboard, you will eventually strike a key that will make one of the objects on the music rack vibrate; then another key for another object, and so on. As this happens, each vibrating object is in resonance with the vibrating piano string struck by the key. The striking of some key may cause all the objects to vibrate at once. If this happens, it will be because the piano string is in resonance with the music rack, and the vibrating rack is bouncing the objects up and down.

The Bible tells us that Joshua, the military leader of the ancient Israelis, led an army against the walled city of Jericho. When the army arrived at the city, Joshua commanded it to march around the walls shouting and blowing on trumpets. The great sound made by the army caused the walls to crumble.

How did Joshua win the Battle of Jericho?

It is interesting to let our imaginations play with this story. Picture an army of tens of thousands of men marching around Jericho's walls in ranks two-score wide. Thousands upon thousands of marching feet all strike the ground at the same time. As each foot strikes the ground, its owner shouts, "Ho!" At the same moment, those soldiers who have trumpets blow an ear-splitting blast. What a deafening sea

of sound rolls toward the walls! Now, suppose the cadence of the marching feet, the shouts and the trumpets are in resonance with the walls. As the waves of sound strike them, the walls begin to tremble. Dust spurts out from between the great stones as the mortar is powdered by vibrations that strike the walls through the ground and the air. At last, the quaking walls crumble beneath the pounding of the thunderous barrage of sound that beats upon them. Maybe it happened that way.

When soldiers march across a bridge, they are ordered to break step. If they continue to march in step, the frequency of their cadence might be in resonance with the bridge, and this would cause the bridge to tremble violently and possibly collapse. Perhaps you have been at a football game when the spectators in the grandstand began to clap their hands in unison. You not only could hear the clapping, but possibly you could also feel the grandstand tremble to the cadence of the sound.

Reflected Sound

A reflected sound is called an *echo*. In

What is an echo?

general, an echo has the same characteristics as the original sound. If you are in a quiet place outdoors and you shout your first name in the direction of a wall, a hill, a cliff or a bluff that is about one hundred paces away, you will hear your name reflected back to you. The echo of your name will sound the same in pitch and diction as when you spoke it, although it will be fainter, because it lost energy during its round trip.

Most bats eat insects. These insects are

Do bats use their eyesight to find insects?

caught while flying in the dark. How bats are able to locate such tiny prey as mosquitoes and gnats in the dark puzzled men for centuries. In 1793, the

22

to his laboratory, where he dissected their stomachs. He found that the blinded bats had just as many insects in their stomachs as did the bats that could see. From this rather cruel experiment, Spallanzani concluded that bats do not hunt insects by sight and, in fact, do not need light to find their way about.

Spallanzani still did not know how bats catch insects in the dark. To investigate further, he made brass tubes, a twenty-fifth of an inch

How do bats locate insects?

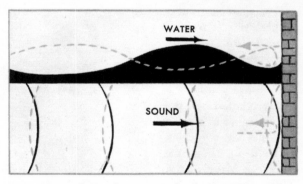

The sound wave of an echo bounces back by reflection, much like water bouncing from a wall.

brilliant Italian scientist Lazzaro Spallanzani became interested in how animals find their prey at night. He learned that owls and certain other night-hunting animals rely on their big eyes to make use of what little light may be available. These creatures became helpless in total darkness. Bats, however, could flit easily through the darkest rooms. Spallanzani blinded some bats. They flew as well as ever. He then put identifying marks on the wings of each bat and released them outdoors. Four days later, he went to the bell tower of the cathedral of Pavia, where he had caught the bats. He climbed into the bell tower at dawn, just when the bats were returning from their night's hunting. He again caught the bats he had blinded. He took them and some others

in diameter. He put these tubes into the ears of bats, and the bats flew about as skillfully as ever. Then he plugged the tiny tubes. Now, the bats flew about clumsily, bumping into every obstacle. Spallanzani concluded that bats somehow used their sense of hearing to locate insects, as well as to fly skillfully among the branches of trees — all in the dark. It was not until nearly one-

and-a-half centuries later that scientists learned how bats perform their marvelous feats of aerial maneuvering.

In 1932, the Dutch zoologist Sven Dijkgraaf found that a faint clicking sound which bats make was connected with the way they locate obstacles. A few years later, the American scientist Donald R. Griffin discovered that bats make a large number of sounds, but all except the faint clicks are of a pitch so high that human beings cannot hear them. Another American scientist, Robert Galambos, showed that covering the mouths of bats, and thereby preventing them from emitting sounds, was just as effective as plugging their ears. This caused them to lose their ability to avoid obstacles when flying in the dark.

Perhaps you have heard bats squeak as they flit about on a summer evening, or perhaps you have heard roosting bats

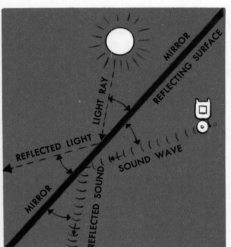

The reflection of sound is much like the reflection of light. When a ray of light strikes a reflecting surface at an angle, the ray is reflected at exactly the same angle. This is true of sound, too. You can prove this by an interesting experiment. Let us suppose you have a toy cricket. Hold the cricket in your cupped hands, which are facing forward at about the level of your chest. Stand about thirty-five paces from a wall, facing the wall at an angle. Ask a friend to stand about forty-five paces from the same wall, on

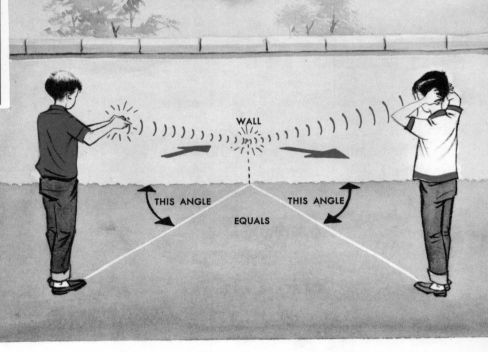

the side toward which you are facing. As you continually click the cricket, ask your friend to walk sideways back and forth, until he finds the place where the clicks sound the loudest. When he finds this place, ask him to cup his hands behind his ears, and then to turn his head back and forth until he finds the position in which the clicks sound the loudest. When he has found this place and position, he should be facing toward a point on the wall midway between you and him. Now, make a mark on the ground right below your cupped hands. Draw a line from this mark to the wall, in the direction toward which your hands were pointing. Ask your friend to draw a line on the ground to the wall, in the direction toward which his nose is pointing. His line should meet the wall at the same point your line did. The line from you to the wall represents the path of the center of the sound waves moving from the cricket to the wall; the line from the wall to your friend represents the path along which the center of the sound waves were reflected from the wall. Since both lines meet the wall at the same angle, the sound waves must have been reflected at the same angle at which they struck the wall.

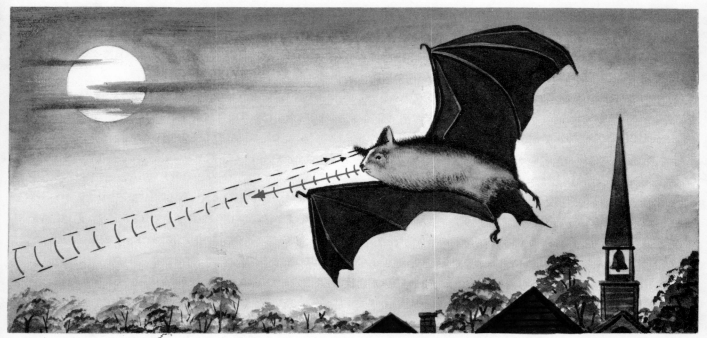

A bat has a "'built-in sonar installation." It sends out sound (dotted line) and receives an echo (broken line), enabling it to tell the distance and location of obstacles and insects.

squeak and chitter as they squabble over places to sleep during the day. Neither the squeaks nor the chittering sounds are the ones used by bats as they hunt insects. If you want to hear the clicking sounds, you can probably do so. On a quiet summer evening, when bats are about, toss tiny pebbles or small wads of wet absorbent cotton gently into the air four or five feet above your head. In this way, you will probably decoy bats to flit near you. As the bats chase your decoy, they will make a faint clicking sound. The clicks are the sounds of lowest pitch of the total sounds the bats are emitting.

But just how do bats use the sounds to help them locate prey? The method they use is called **How do bats use sound?** *echo-location*. As a bat flies about, it continually emits high-pitched sounds. These sounds have a frequency of 5,000 to 120,000 cycles per second. You will remember that one cycle is one complete vibration. The sounds last from 1/1,000 to 1/2,000 of a second, and they are repeated ten to twenty times a second. When these sounds strike an insect, they bounce back to the bat's ears. Then, the bat increases the number of sounds it emits, sending forth as many as 250 sounds per second. Following the path of the echoes, the bat closes in upon its insect prey. The bats' method of echo-location is very much like radar, except that bats use sound waves, while radar uses a kind of radio wave.

The wonderful precision of the bats' echo-location method is made apparent when you consider how faint is the echo that returns to a bat from an insect as small as a mosquito or a gnat — and that at the same time, echoes are also returning to the bat from twigs, leaves, blades of grass and other obstacles. The American brown bat weighs only about

25

one-quarter of an ounce. In a night's hunting, this little bat catches insects whose total weight is equal to its own. Scientists have found that this means the bat catches a mosquito every six seconds, all through the night.

Certain birds also use echo-location. So

How does the porpoise use sound to catch fish in the sea?

do animals that live in the sea. Two scientists experimented with a porpoise, one of the animals that locates its prey by echo-location. The scientists found that a porpoise has a vocabulary of grunts, whistles, squeals, clicks and rasping sounds. However, the sound that the porpoise uses for echo-location is a sort of creak. In a muddy pond on a pitch-dark night, the porpoise was able to echo-locate a six-inch fish held in the water by a scientist. This feat is even more remarkable when you know that the part of the fish's body from which the creaks echoed back to the porpoise was the fish's swim-bladder, an air-filled sac only about an inch in diameter.

Perhaps you have seen a blind person

How do people who are blind locate objects?

walking on a busy street almost as well as a person who can see. It has been known for a long time that some blind persons develop a seemingly new sense to take the place of their lost sight. When questioned about this "sense," blind persons said they could just "feel" or "know" the presence of objects nearby. Some said it was their face, some said it was their forehead, and still others said it was their hands that gave them the feeling that they were near an object.

In a series of experiments, scientists covered first the face, then the forehead, then the hands and then the ears of each blind person with whom they worked. It was not until the ears were covered that a blind person lost his ability to detect objects in front of himself. Just as in the case of Spallanzani's bats, this experiment proved that hearing is the sense that blind persons substitute for their lost sight. But scientists have not yet learned exactly what sounds blind persons use for echo-location.

When submarines were first used in

How do ships locate enemy submarines?

warfare, anti-submarine ships found themselves confronted with the problem of locating an enemy ship that could remain completely concealed beneath the sea. To solve this problem, scientists developed an underwater electrical echo-locator that was later called *sonar*.

At first, sensitive sound-receiving devices were lowered beneath the surface of the ocean, and the anti-submarine ships simply tried to hear the sounds of the submarine. This idea had some success, but the submarine did not always oblige by making distinguishable sounds. Also, the sounds of the listening ship's own engines or the engines of ships being escorted interfered with sounds that might be those of a submarine.

An improved device consisted of both an instrument that could send out powerful sound waves and a sensitive listening instrument. The first instrument sent out a beam of short pulses of sound, and the second instrument picked up any echo that might have resulted from sound pulses striking an underwater obstacle — such as a submarine. Modern sonar sends out sound as powerful as six million loud shouts and can locate a submarine several miles away.

Still another improvement in submarine detection is being developed in the United States — one that may make possible the detection of enemy undersea craft thousands of miles away. The program, known as Project Artemis, makes use of a giant underwater sound generator to convert electric waves

into sound waves. Hydrophones are placed at different sea depths to pick up the sound waves from objects in the ocean.

Sonar has found peaceful uses. It is used to determine the depth of water in which ships are moving. Before sonar, depth was found by throwing overboard a weighted line, known as a lead line. At every few feet, the lead line had either a knot or a ring of lead.

By measuring the time that a sound wave takes to travel to an obstacle and back, we can figure out the distance of the object. The ship, equipped with sonar, locates the submarine on this principle.

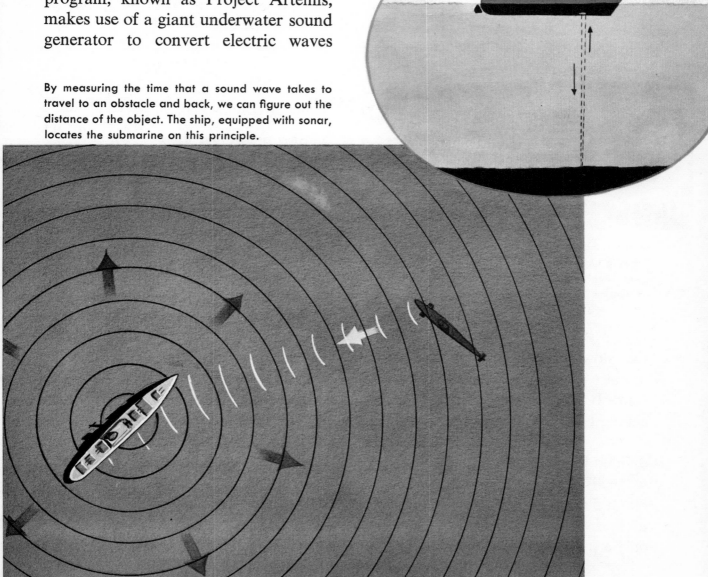

When the weight touched bottom, the line was hauled up, the knots or rings were counted and the depth of the water was known from the length of the line that had been underwater. Compare

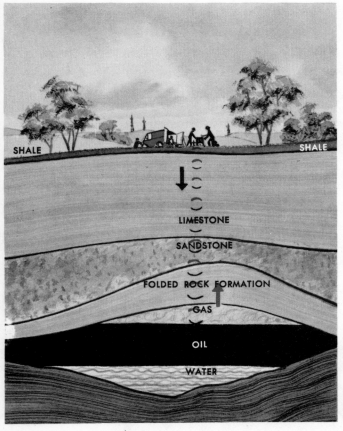

SHALE   SHALE
LIMESTONE
SANDSTONE
FOLDED ROCK FORMATION
GAS
OIL
WATER

Shown is a cutaway view of an oil deposit in the earth, showing typical echo patterns that enable the geologist to locate the presence of the precious commodity, as well as the best location to drill for it. A seismograph records the echo patterns.

this slow process with sonar. A sound impulse is sent out from the ship's bottom. It strikes the sea bottom and echoes back to the ship. The time taken by the sound impulse's round trip is divided by two — and the depth of the water is known. Since sound travels about 5,000 feet a second in sea water, to find depth by sonar usually takes only a fraction of a second.

Fishermen found that they could use

How are echoes used to detect schools of fish? sonar to locate schools of fish, for as we have learned, sound is reflected

from the swim bladders of fish. When fishermen have determined the location of the school, nets can be cast with accuracy. If you do not send out any sound impulses, you can use sonar simply to listen to underwater sounds.

Sailors listening with sonar have been amazed to learn that the creatures of the sea are not silent as was previously believed. Toadfish make a sound like a base drum, the squirrelfish grinds its teeth to make a sound like a rusty hinge, and certain rockfish grunt. A bed of shrimp sounds like fat sizzling on a fire.

Geologists have learned that vibrations

How are echoes used to locate minerals? travel through various kinds of rock and

soil at varying speeds, and that vibrations are reflected strongly by hard rock and weakly by soft rock and soil. This knowledge gives geologists a method by which to prospect for minerals beneath the surface of the earth without digging. They use an instrument, called a *seismograph*, to record vibrations sent through the earth from small explosions set off in an area. The seismograph tells the travel-time and strength of the vibrations. From this data, geologists can tell through what kinds of rock the vibrations passed and from what kinds they were reflected. They also know what echo patterns indicate the presence of rocks in which oil and many other valuable minerals are found.

Musical Sounds and Musical Instruments

What is musical sound?

Most of us would say that music is the sound made by a band, or an orchestra or by a musical instrument. We would say that music is the sound made by a chorus of singers or one person singing alone. We would probably consider music to be the sounds we make when blowing into a tin whistle, or moaning into a kazoo or when singing in the shower or bathtub. In short, we ordinarily consider any pleasing series of sounds to be musical.

A scientist would not deny us our definition of a musical sound, but he would require a more precise definition for his work. He would say that a musical sound is one whose wave pattern is regular; that is, the waves are evenly-spaced and all have the same amplitude. You will remember that amplitude of sound waves is a measure of their loudness. The sound made by a tuning fork is a good example of a musical sound. So is the sound of a siren.

We will better understand a musical sound if we learn what noise is. Ordinarily, we would say that noise is any

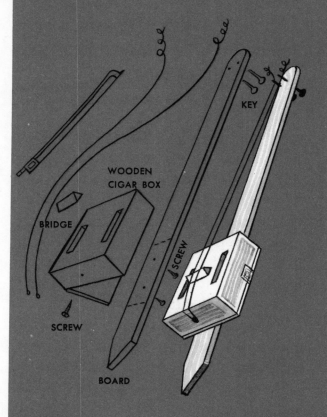

HOW YOU CAN MAKE A GUITAR OR A VIOLONCELLO

With a pocket knife, cut two rectangular holes in the bottom of a cigar box. Obtain a board about twenty inches long, two inches wide and three-quarters of an inch thick. Saw out a two-inch section at one end, and fasten the board to the bottom of the box with small bolts. Fasten the lid shut. Whittle two violin pegs, or buy them at a music store. In the middle of the free end of the board, drill holes into which the pegs fit tightly. Whittle a triangular piece of wood for a bridge. Run two guitar strings from screws at the end of the box, over the bridge and to the pegs. Wind the strings tight. Now you can strum tunes on your guitar. If you use a board about four feet long, and fasten the cigar box a foot from one end and use violin strings, you will have a violoncello upon which you can play with a violin bow.

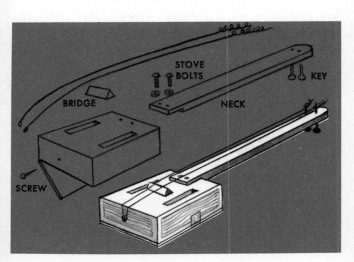

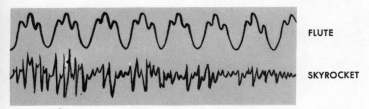

FLUTE

SKYROCKET

Sound waves that show a regular pattern (top) have a pleasing sound, while unpleasant sounds are produced by things that vibrate irregularly.

sound we don't like. For instance, probably everyone dislikes the screech of automobile brakes, and we would call this sound noise. But the sound waves that make up the screech may have a regular pattern. A scientist, then, however much he may dislike the screech, would have to call it a musical sound, according to his definition.

Suppose you are talking on the telephone, while your sister in the same room is practicing her singing lesson. If you have difficulty hearing what is being said to you on the phone, you will consider your sister's singing to be noise, even though every note she sings may be a pure musical sound. Here, again, a common idea about sound conflicts with the scientific definition.

However, we still have to be given a scientific definition of noise. From what we have already learned, you can probably guess that, scientifically, noise is sound made by an irregular pattern of waves. When you stamp your foot on the pavement, drop a book or clap your hands, the sound you make is noise.

Man was making music long before he
What is a musical scale?
began to study it. He sang, stamped and clapped his hands. Probably some prehistoric hunter who found the twang of his bowstring pleasing, experimented with stretched strings until he invented the first musical instrument. Archaeologists — persons who dig up buried cities to study the civilizations that built them — have found crude lyres that were made by stretching strings of different length across bent tree branches.

The ancient Greeks, who played on lyres and other stringed musical instruments, were the first to study music scientifically. Their musicians established a series of sounds of ascending and descending pitch; that is, a scale of musical notes.

The Greek scientists learned that if a tightly stretched string produces a sound of a certain pitch, then a string half as long produces a sound with a pitch exactly eight notes — called an *octave* — higher on the musical scale. A string half as long as the second one produces a pitch eight more notes higher. In short, they learned that if the length of a vibrating string is halved, its pitch is doubled.

The keys of a piano produce sounds of different pitch. In the musical notes (above) and on the piano (below) is a scale in which the last tone is one octave higher than the first.

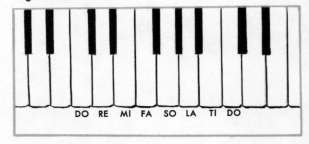

DO RE MI FA SO LA TI DO

The Greeks also learned that a taut string produces a higher pitch than a loose string, and a thin string produces a higher pitch than a thick one. They did not understand the reasons for all these facts. Since the time of the Greeks, we have learned that pitch depends on frequency. This fact explains what the Greeks learned about vibrating strings. If we measure the frequency of short, tight or thin vibrating strings, we find it is higher than the frequency of long, loose or thick strings.

Any musical sound is made by vibrations twice as fast as those of a sound that is an octave lower, and half as fast as those of a sound that is an octave higher. Middle C has a frequency of 256 cycles per second; the next lower C has a frequency of 128; and the C next higher to middle C has a frequency of 512.

An octave actually includes thirteen tones or musical notes — eight whole notes and five half notes. On a piano the white keys represent whole notes, the black keys half notes. To move from one white key to the next is to move from one whole note to the next. To move from a white key to a black key, or from black to white, is to move one half note.

When two or more musical notes sounded at the same time **What is harmony?** produce a pleasing sound, we say they are in *harmony*. When the sound is displeasing, we say the notes are in *discord*. Scientists have discovered that harmony de-

HOW TO MAKE A HARP

Nail three pieces of board together in the form of a triangle. Obtain eight or ten rubber bands, and break each rubber band so that you can pull it out into a single length. Stretch the rubber bands tightly, and fasten them to the sides of the wooden triangle with thumbtacks. You have made a harp on which you can play tunes by plucking the rubber bands. Another way of making a harp is by gluing a right-angled triangle to the bottom of a wooden cigar box, and stringing the rubber bands as shown in the drawing below. Your harp also illustrates that the length and pitch of a vibrating string are related. You will hear that the short rubber bands produce a higher tone than the long ones.

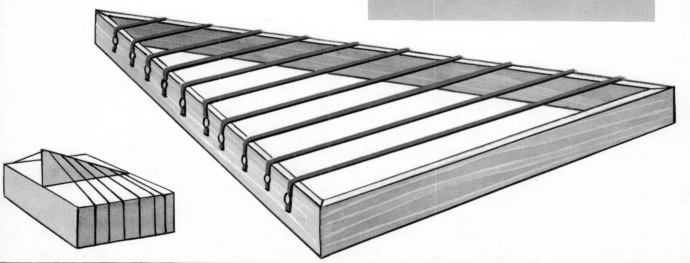

HOW TO MAKE A MILK-BOTTLE ORGAN

You can make an organ from bottles and water. Obtain eight empty soda bottles. Place them in a row. Put a little water in the bottom of the first bottle and a little more water in the second bottle. In the third bottle, put an amount of water that is slightly more than that in the second bottle. Continue to put water in the bottles until the eighth bottle is about two-thirds full. Blow your breath across the top of each bottle in turn. You will see that the more water there is in a bottle, the higher a note it produces. By removing or adding a little water to the bottles, you can make them produce a musical scale. Then, by blowing your breath across their tops, you can play tunes. If you become tired blowing your breath, you can move air across the tops of the bottles by using a vacuum cleaner hose.

HOW TO MAKE A WATER-TROMBONE

To make a trombone, fill a bottle with water to about two inches from the top. A soda bottle will do very well. Put a drinking straw into the bottle. Hold the straw steady with one hand and move the bottle up and down with the other hand, while you blow your breath across the top of the straw. The pitch of the sound emitted by the straw will vary according to how much of the straw is in the water. This is so because the amount of water in the straw determines the length of the vibrating air column above it.

HOW TO MAKE A NAIL-PIANO

Drive eight thin nails into a board in a row, three-quarters of an inch apart. Drive each nail a little farther into the board than the nail preceding it. Push another nail into the end of a cork or a small piece of wood. Use this nail to strike the other nails in the board. The shorter the nail, the higher the pitch of a sound it will produce. You can play tunes on your nail-piano.

HOW TO MAKE A XYLOPHONE

To make a xylophone, you will need eight pieces of hard wood, such as broom handles are made of. Cut the pieces to the following lengths: 10, 9 ½, 9, 8 ¾, 8 ½, 7 ¾, 7 ¼ and 7 inches. Tie the pieces of wood together with strings, as shown. You can play a tune on your xylophone by striking the wooden bars with another stick of hard wood. If you want to tune your xylophone, cut a little off the end of a bar to raise its pitch, or whittle a little from the middle of a bar to lower its tone.

HOW TO MAKE A SLIDE-WHISTLE

You can make a slide-whistle from a piece of bamboo. Cut a notch in the bamboo tube near one end. Whittle a piece of soft wood into the shape of a cylinder, which will fit into the tube. Then, shave off one side of the cylinder to make it flat. Place the cylinder into the tube above the notch. When you blow into this end of the tube, you will hear a whistle as the air goes out of the notch and makes the column of air in the tube vibrate. Whittle another cylinder of soft wood — this one to fit loosely in the tube. Glue the cylinder to the head of a nail or to the eraser of a pencil. Insert the cylinder into the open end of your whistle. By sliding this cylinder up and down the tube, you can change the pitch of your slide-whistle, as you vary the length of the vibrating column of air within the tube.

pends on the frequencies of the notes that sound together. For example, the notes C, E and G are in harmony, and their respective frequencies are 256, 320 and 384. If you divide these frequencies by the common denominator 64, you obtain the numbers 4, 5, 6, respectively. Any three notes whose frequencies bear the relationship of 4:5:6 will be in harmony — for instance, A, C♯ and E. Many other frequencies besides those related by 4:5:6 are in harmony. The rule is that tones whose frequencies are related by any combination of the small whole numbers 1:2:3:4:5:6:7:8 are in harmony. Notes in harmony are said to form a *chord*.

If you were to strike on a piano mid-

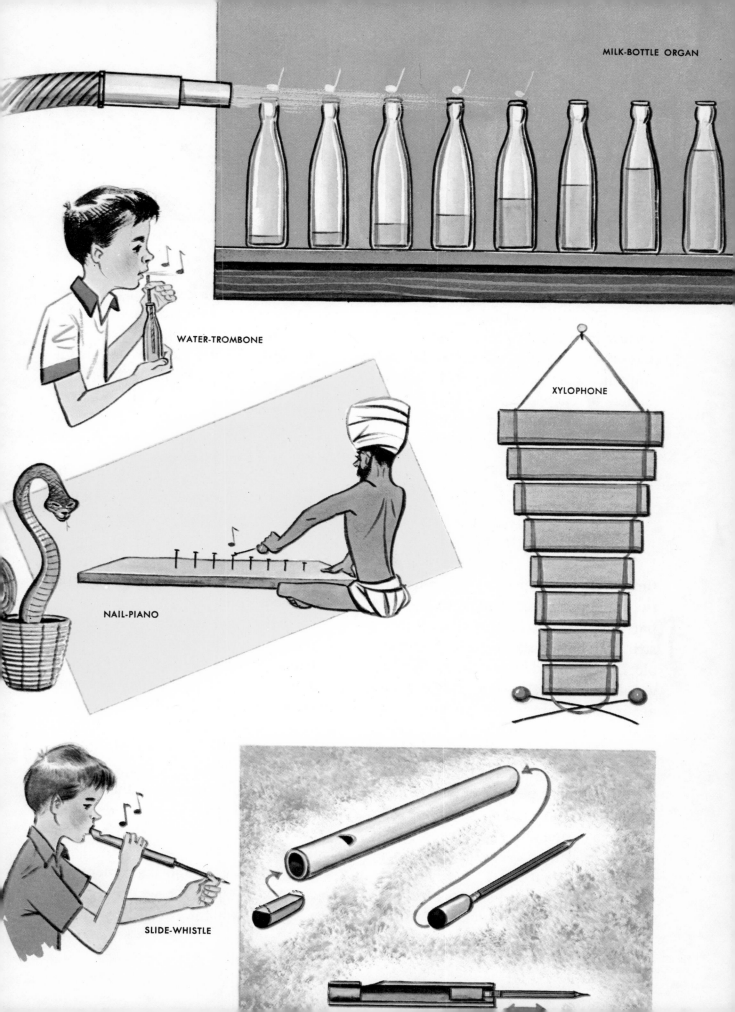

MILK-BOTTLE ORGAN

WATER-TROMBONE

XYLOPHONE

NAIL-PIANO

SLIDE-WHISTLE

dle C and C♯, the resulting sound would not be pleasant. Keeping in mind what we just learned, we can easily see why these two notes produce discord. Their frequencies are 256 and 271 and are related to each other as 4:4⅕. Since these are not both whole numbers, the sound they produce is a discord.

You probably know of many stringed instruments. The

How do stringed instruments produce sound? violin, cello, guitar, banjo, zither and harp are some of them. All these instruments consist of two main parts: the strings, and another part that vibrates in resonance with the strings to enrich their sound. For example, the violin is a box of thin wood over which strings are stretched. The strings are made to vibrate by plucking or by drawing a bow over them. The strings vary in tautness and thickness. In the harp and zither the strings are of different lengths. The performer on a stringed instrument can change the pitch of a string by pressing his finger on it, thereby varying the length of the vibrating part of the string.

Thus, by the use of strings of varying length, tautness and thickness, tone of a great variety of pitch may be produced by stringed instruments.

Wind instruments include the trombone, trumpet, bu-

How do wind instruments produce sound? gle, tuba, flute, piccolo, clarinet and saxophone. A wind instrument is constructed so that blowing breath into it causes a column of air inside to vibrate. The frequency of the vibration depends on the frequency of the air column. The shorter the air column, the higher the frequency, and hence, the higher the pitch of the instrument.

The lengths of vibrating air columns —and consequently the pitch—of wind instruments may be varied by opening and closing holes at different locations. This is the way it is done in the flute, piccolo, clarinet and saxophone. In the trombone, the length of the air column is varied by sliding a U-shaped hollow pipe back and forth; and in the trumpet and French horn, finger valves block parts of the air column to vary its length.

The pitch of a wind instrument also varies according to the width of the vibrating air column. In an organ, the long, wide pipes make low-pitched sounds, and the short, narrow pipes make high-pitched sounds.

A percussion instrument is one that pro-

How do percussion instruments produce sound?

duces a musical sound when struck in a particular manner. A drum, xylophone, triangle, bell and cymbals are all percussion instruments.

Of course, we know how these instruments produce musical sounds, because we have learned how any struck object vibrates and produces sound waves. The resonant vibration of air within a drum amplifies the sound made by the vibrating drumhead. A piano is a combination of percussion and stringed instruments. Striking a piano key causes a felt hammer to strike strings of different lengths within the piano.

Living Sound Organs

One of the most remarkable instru-

What is the human voice?

ments is the human voice. Its variation in quality is greater than that of any musical instrument. Voice sounds are produced by the vibration of two ligaments, called the *vocal cords*. They are stretched across the larynx (or "Adam's apple") in such a manner as to leave only a narrow slit between them for the passage of air. Air from the lungs passes through the narrow slit and causes the vocal cords to vibrate.

Muscles attached to the vocal cords may increase their pull on the ligaments, thereby tightening and thinning them; or else they may relax their tension, thereby loosening and thickening the ligaments.

We have learned that a tight, thin cord has a higher pitch than a loose, thick one. This principle holds for vocal cords, too. When the vocal cords are tight and thin, the voice is high; when the vocal cords are loose and thick, the voice is low. We also learned that a

Cut a wide rubber band into two equal lengths. Place the two pieces side by side, and grip them firmly between the thumb and forefinger of each hand. Stretch them tight. Touch your lips with the stretched rubber bands, and blow your breath through them. The sound they produce is due to their vibration. You can vary the pitch of this sound by the degree to which you stretch the rubber bands. The rubber bands produce sound in much the same way that your vocal cords do. Muscles stretch the vocal cords to change the pitch of your voice.

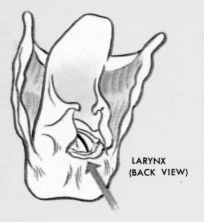

LARYNX
(BACK VIEW)

BULLFROG

KATYDID

VOCAL CORDS
DURING
BREATHING

VOCAL CORDS
DURING
SPEAKING

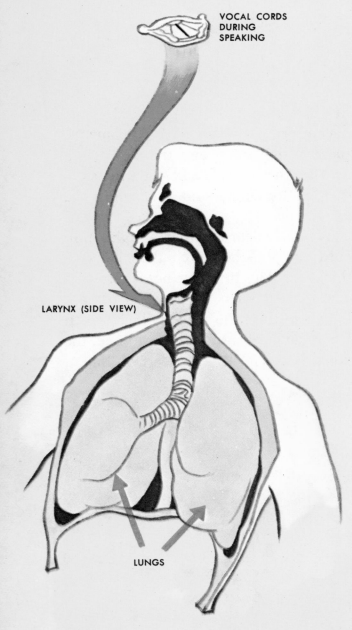

LARYNX (SIDE VIEW)

LUNGS

short vibrating cord has a higher pitch than a long one. So, we should not be surprised to learn that the vocal cords of women are about one-half inch long and those of men are about three-quarters of an inch long. Now you know why the voices of babies are so high — because they have very short vocal cords.

The range between the lowest and highest pitch of the same set of vocal cords is about two-and-a-half octaves.

Of course, vocal cords do not simply make sounds by themselves. They are attached to muscles that enable the owner of the vocal cords to control their actions at will.

The quality of the voice depends upon the manner in which its tones are modified by resonating the cavities of the mouth and nose. You can easily prove this by holding your nostrils closed while you are talking. Note the thinness of your voice. Then remove your fingers and note how much richer your voice is. Also ask a friend to do the same, so that you can hear how resonance increases the richness of his voice.

All the sounds of our speech are not

The human voice organs are the most versatile "sound instruments" in the world.

BIRD

BEE

Although very many kinds of animals make sounds, not all have vocal cords. The dog's bark, the cow's moo, the cat's meow and the sounds of other mammals are made by means of vocal cords. Birds sing, squawk, peep, whistle and chatter by means of a ring of cartilage, called a syrinx, in the bird's windpipe. A male katydid has a file-like row of ridges on one of its wings. When the katydid rubs part of the other wing against this file, sounds are produced that seem to say "katy-did, katy-did," or "she didn't, she didn't." A bee's hum is made by the rapid motion of its wings, causing the surrounding air to vibrate. To increase the loudness of its croaks, a bullfrog may puff up its throat like a balloon. The distended throat acts as a resonator that magnifies the sound made by the frog's vocal cords.

made by our vocal cords. For example, when we say a word that contains the letter *t*, we make a slight clicking sound by suddenly pulling the tongue away from the roof of the mouth just behind the front teeth. To make *b* and *p* sounds, we cause an explosion of air through our lips. The *s* is a hissing sound.

Although musical instruments may have a greater range, none has the capability of expression of the human voice. A voice may be soft, harsh, nasal, throaty; friendly, angry, commanding, cajoling, whining; and have a hundred other shades, meanings and qualities.

Everyone knows we hear with our ears.

How do we hear? But it is worthwhile to understand how these wonderful organs work. The human ear may be divided into three main parts: the *outer ear*, the *middle ear* and the *inner ear*. The outer ear consists of the part on the outside of the head (made of cartilage), and also the *auditory canal*. The cartilaginous part of the ear helps to direct sound waves into the auditory canal, a passageway through which sounds reach

The human ear receives the sound waves around us. The illustration on the right is a cross section of the ear showing its various parts.

SEMICIRCULAR CANALS   MIDDLE EAR

HAMMER

ANVIL

OUTER EAR

INNER EAR

COCHLEA

STIRRUP

AUDITORY CANAL

AUDITORY NERVE

EARDRUM

EUSTACHIAN TUBE

the middle ear. Stretching across the inner end of the auditory canal and completely blocking it is a circular membrane, the *eardrum*. Inward from the eardrum is the middle ear.

Touching the inner surface of the eardrum is a tiny bone, the *malleus,* or hammer. The malleus connects by a joint to another little bone, the *incus,* or anvil. And the incus is joined to a third little bone, the *stapes,* or stirrup — so named because it looks like a stirrup. These three bones stretch across the cavity of the middle ear, from front to back. The lower part of the middle ear opens upon the *Eustachian tube* that leads to the throat. Because of this tube, air pressure in the middle ear can be equalized with air pressure outside the eardrum.

The stapes touches a snail-shaped tube called the *cochlea*. The cochlea opens upon three thin tubes, the *semicircular canals*. Both the cochlea and the semicircular canals are filled with liquid. Inward from the cochlea, the *auditory nerve* leads to the brain.

When sound waves strike the eardrum and cause it to vibrate, the eardrum causes the malleus to vibrate, too.

The malleus strikes against the incus with each vibration. The incus passes the vibration to the stapes. These three tiny bones serve to multiply by more than twenty times the strength of vibrations of the eardrum.

The footplate of the stapes passes the vibrations to the liquid in the inner ear. Here, the vibrations press upon certain tissues, called *organs of Corti*. These organs change the pressure into nerve impulses that are carried to the brain by the auditory nerve. The brain interprets the impulses as sound.

This complicated system works very well. It can make you aware of a very wide range and complex combination of sound, such as that which reaches your ear from an orchestra. The ear can transmit vibrations to the brain having frequencies of from 20 cycles to 20,000 cycles per second. Children may be able to hear sound of more than 30,000 cycles per second. At 2,000 cycles per second, the human ear may be able to hear sounds so faint that they have an amplitude of less than 1/500,000,000 of an inch — about one-half the diameter of the hydrogen atom, the smallest of all atoms.

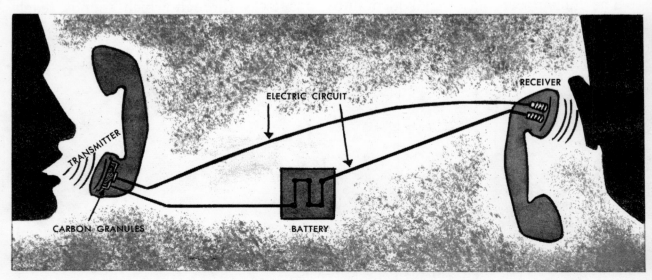

ELECTRIC CIRCUIT

RECEIVER

TRANSMITTER

CARBON GRANULES

BATTERY

Sound and Communication

A telephone does not really carry sound.

How does a telephone carry sound? How, then, can a person at one end of a telephone line hear voices, music or any other sound made at the other end? A telephone has two main parts. One is the *mouthpiece,* or *transmitter,* and the other is the *receiver.* You speak into the transmitter and hold the receiver to your ear.

Inside the transmitter is a small round box filled with grains of carbon. The top of this box is a thin metal disk, called a *diaphragm.* When you talk into the transmitter, the sound waves produced by your voice cause the diaphragm to vibrate. The back-and-forth movements of the diaphragm alternately press the carbon grains together and then leave them room to spread apart.

There is an electric circuit in the telephone wires that runs between your phone and the phone of the person to whom you are talking. When the diaphragm presses the carbon grains together, more electric current flows in

the circuit; when the grains are farther apart, less current flows. Thus, the amount of electric current in a telephone circuit varies from moment to moment as the diaphragm vibrates.

In the receiver is another diaphragm. This diaphragm rests on a magnet. The strength with which this magnet pulls on the diaphragm varies in proportion to the amount of electric current. When the pull is strong, the diaphragm moves toward the magnet, and when the pull is weak, the diaphragm springs away from the magnet. The back-and-forth movements of the diaphragm generate air waves that reach your ear as sound. Because the vibrations of the diaphragm in the transmitter control the flow of current, they produce identical vibrations of the diaphragm in the receiver. Thus, the sound waves that leave the receiver are identical with those that enter the transmitter. As a result, you can hear sound coming from the receiver just as though the sound had traveled along the wire.

A microphone in a broadcasting studio

How does a radio transmit sound without wires? is constructed very much like a transmitter of a telephone. Sound waves entering the microphone cause it to vary electrical impulses. These impulses, instead of flowing

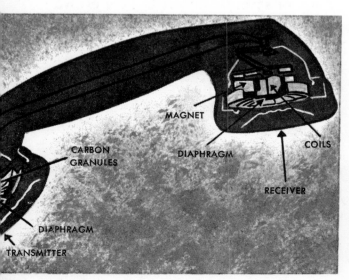

CARBON GRANULES

MAGNET

DIAPHRAGM

COILS

RECEIVER

DIAPHRAGM

TRANSMITTER

At left is a cutaway view of the handpiece of a modern telephone, showing the principal parts of the transmitter and receiver. The diagram next to it shows a simple telephone circuit with a battery. (After diagrams, courtesy Bell Telephone Laboratories.)

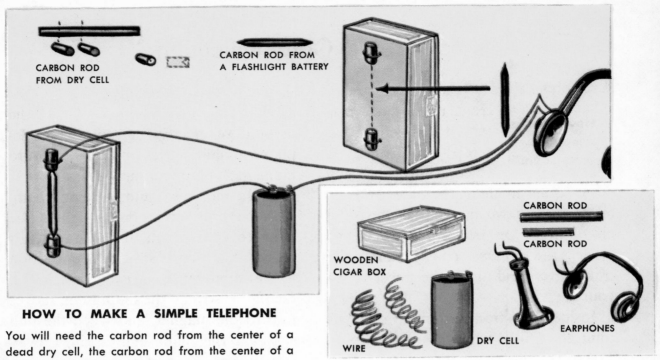

HOW TO MAKE A SIMPLE TELEPHONE

You will need the carbon rod from the center of a dead dry cell, the carbon rod from the center of a flashlight battery, a cigar box, a live dry cell, wires and an old telephone receiver or a set of earphones. Saw off two one-inch lengths of the carbon rod from the dead dry cell, and grind out a small hollow in the end of each piece. With sandpaper, sharpen the ends of the rod from the flashlight battery. Affix the two hollowed-out pieces of carbon to the back of the cigar box, using wire in the manner shown. The sharpened carbon rod should be placed between the two pieces of carbon, so that its points touch the hollowed-out place in each piece. Fasten a long piece of bell wire to each of the hollowed-out pieces of carbon, and run one wire to one pole of the live dry cell. Run the other wire to another room, where you connect it to the telephone receiver or headphones. Take a third wire and connect the other pole of the dry cell with the receiver, as the illustration shows. Your telephone is complete. If someone talks into the front of the cigar box, the movement of the sharpened carbon rod will vary the amount of electric current in the wires, and the diaphragm of the receiver will vibrate to produce the same sound waves as those of the person speaking into the box.

through wires to a receiver, go to electronic equipment that transforms them into electromagnetic, or radio, waves. These waves are broadcast. When the waves reach a radio, other electronic devices change the radio waves to electrical impulses. These impulses are transformed into sound waves by the radio's speaker, which works on the same principle as a telephone receiver.

Not very long ago, a famous speech, a brilliant performance by a musician or the clever words of a little child could be heard once — and

How can we record sound?

then were lost to our ears forever. Of course, you know that nowadays we can hear over and over again any sounds we choose — if we record them in any of several ways. But how do we go about recording sounds? In 1877, the American inventor Thomas Alva Edison wrapped tin foil about a wooden cylinder. The cylinder was arranged so that it could be turned by a crank attached to one end. Edison also attached a needle to one side of a metal diaphragm and rested the needle on the tin-foil cylinder. The other side of the diaphragm rested on a large horn.

While Edison turned the crank, he

shouted into the horn, "Mary had a little lamb!" The sound waves of his voice made the diaphragm vibrate. The diaphragm moved the attached needle up and down and cut grooves into the tin foil.

When Edison had finished his recitation, he put the needle at the beginning of the grooves and again turned the crank. Now, the needle bumped along the same grooves and the diaphragm vibrated, producing sound waves. As a result, the first phonograph repeated in a faint, tinny voice, "Mary had a little lamb."

Within ten years, tin-foil cylinders had been replaced by wax cylinders, and these, in turn, had given way to flat disks, such as we use today. Also, a way had been found to cut grooves in sidewise zigzags, instead of up-and-down bumps.

In the 1920's electronic principles were applied to phonograph recording. This is the method used today. Sound enters a microphone and is changed into electrical impulses. These impulses vary the strength of a magnet that controls the disk-cutting needle. The disk that is cut by the recording needle is called the master disk. It is electrically covered with a thin coating of metal, and it is used as a mold from which to make many other disks.

Put a record on a turntable and start the phonograph running. Place your fingernail lightly on the grooves of the record. You will hear sound coming from your fingernail, and you will also feel the sound as the vibrations produced by the motion of your fingernail are transmitted along the bones of your arm.

With a magnifying glass, examine the grooves in a phonograph record. Note how they wiggle back and forth. As the disk turns, the phonograph needle runs along the groove, wiggling back and forth as it follows the turnings and twistings of the groove.

Push a needle through a corner of a clean milk carton. Hold the needle in the grooves of a record turning on a turntable. You will find that the carton acts as a resonator that magnifies the vibrations of the needle, so that you can hear sound coming from the record. Use caution to avoid damage to the record.

Electronic equipment is also used to cause the phonograph disk to reproduce sound from the zigzags cut in it. The phonograph needle is attached to a device much like a telephone transmitter. The zigzag motion of the needle, as the grooves run beneath it, is changed into electrical impulses. These varying impulses vary the strength of a magnet in a speaker, and sound issues from the speaker, just as it does in a radio.

Our two ears cause us to hear sound

What is stereophonic sound?

more richly and vividly than if we had just one ear. Two ears give sound a quality of direction and depth. You can easily prove this by holding a hand tightly over one ear while you listen to any sounds, perhaps music. You will find that music heard through one ear lacks a feeling of depth and is less vivid than the same music heard through both ears.

If only one microphone is used to make a recording, it is similar to listening with one ear. If, on the other hand, separate microphones are used to record sounds that come from the right and from the left, the situation is similar to listening with two ears. When two microphones are used, the needle cuts a separate set of zigzags in each side of the groove it is making — one set for the sound coming to each microphone.

When a disk recorded in this manner is played on a phonograph, the needle reproduces sound separately from the zigzags on each side of the groove. The electrical impulses generated in this way flow to two speakers, each speaker receiving impulses from one side of the

groove. The resulting sound has a quality of depth, so that you feel as though you were in the room in which the sound was recorded.

In a wire recorder, we again use a micro-

How does a wire or tape recorder work?

phone to change sound waves to varying electrical impulses; and, again, the impulses vary the strength of a magnet. Moving past the magnet is a wire that unwinds from one reel and winds on another, as the reels are turned by an electric motor. The moving wire is magnetized, and the amount of magnetization on any part of the wire depends on the strength of the magnet at the moment the wire passed it. In this way, sound waves are translated into lengths of wire, magnetized to varying strengths.

In order to take sound off the magnetized wire, the wire is rewound on the original reel, and then, by means of switches in the recorder, a new electrical circuit is set up. Now, as the wire moves past the magnet, the wire's vary-

ing magnetic strength causes electrical impulses to vary the strength of a magnet in a speaker. The speaker changes the varying strength of the magnet into sound, just as it does in a telephone receiver, or a radio or phonograph speaker.

A tape recorder works the same way as a wire recorder, but instead of a wire, it uses a tape made of two plastic ribbons. Sandwiched between the ribbons is powdered iron, a metal that is very easily magnetized.

Tape recorders also have medical uses. Doctors may record heart beats on tape recorders, and then they can listen to their patients' heart beats at any time. These tapes are kept as part of the medical record.

In making sound movies, we once again use a microphone **How are sound movies made?** to change sound waves into electrical impulses. This time, the varying electrical impulses vary the brightness of a light bulb. A strip on one side of the film moves past the light bulb at the same time that the action is being photographed on the film. When the film is developed, the strip on the side bears varying light and dark areas. They are due to the varying amount of light that reached the film from the light bulb. On a phonograph record, sound is represented by the zigzag grooves; on a tape recorder, sound is represented by lengths of different magnetization; and on a sound-movie film, sound is represented by light and dark areas on a strip at one side. This strip is called the *sound track*.

When a sound movie is projected, the sound track moves past a light bulb whose light shines through the film. The light and dark areas on the sound track vary the amount of light that passes through the film. The varying light strikes an electronic device that changes light into electrical impulses. The electrical impulses, of varying strength, enter a speaker and are changed into sound waves.

Thus, as the picture of people or things photographed on the film is projected on a screen, the sounds made at the time of photographing come from the speaker at the same time. In this way, the voice of an actor, who was speaking when he was photographed, can be heard as we see him move about the movie screen.

The sound track of a movie is synchronized with pictures on the same film.

Ultrasonics and Supersonics

What is ultrasonics?

Ultrasonics concerns sound waves — or more accurately, longitudinal waves — that have a frequency higher than what we ordinarily consider to be the highest frequency of sound waves. Ultrasonic waves are usually considered to begin at 20,000 cycles per second. This, as we have learned, is the upper limit for hearing for most human beings, but, as we also know, children can hear sounds of more than 30,000 cycles per second. So, the 20,000-cycle limit for ultrasonic waves is really not an accurate one. Ultrasonic vibrations of more than a million cycles per second have been produced.

Have you ever seen the dog whistles that you cannot hear? When one of these whistles is blown, no sound seems to come from it. The whistle produces ultrasonic waves that a human being cannot hear, but which a dog can hear. Many other animals hear vibrations that are ultrasonic to human beings. For instance, bats can hear vibrations as high as 145,000 cycles per second.

How can you wash dishes with sound?

By causing ultrasonic vibrations to pass through water in which there are dirty dishes, the particles of food can literally be shaken right off the dishes. There

Scientists have studied shock-wave patterns and plane speeds in special wind tunnels, and thus, have helped to develop better planes.

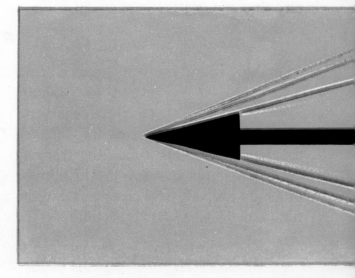

When a whip is flicked rapidly, the tip moves with supersonic speed.

are dishwashers that work this way. Dried blood and other matter are cleaned from surgical and dental instruments by means of ultrasonic vibrations.

When any object moves faster than sound in air, we say that the object is moving with *supersonic* speed. To move through air with supersonic speed requires a great amount of energy. Let us take an airplane for an example. As the plane moves, it pushes air ahead of itself in a series of waves. You probably have seen water waves being pushed forward and outward from the bow of a boat moving through water. Similar waves of air move ahead and outward from the nose of a plane. As the plane flies faster and faster, it catches up with its nose waves and pushes each wave against the one ahead of it. This results in a gathering of compressed air ahead of the plane. Two waves produce twice as much compression as one wave, and ten waves produce ten times as much. To push this mass of compressed air ahead

What is the sound barrier?

of itself, the plane requires a great amount of energy. At the speed of sound — 1,100 feet per second, or 750 miles per hour — the wall of air being pushed before the plane is called the *sound barrier*.

Needle-nose jet and rocket planes are sufficiently powerful to reach, and pass through, the sound barrier. At 750 miles per hour, the nose waves of an airplane, having reached the speed of sound, suddenly become sound waves. At this moment, the powerful compression wave that moves outward from the plane's nose can be heard as a loud explosive sound, called the *sonic boom*.

What is a sonic boom?

Soldiers serving in rifle-range target pits hear the loud crack of bullets passing over the pits. This sound is made by the nose waves of the bullets, which are traveling considerably faster than sound. When a whip is flicked rapidly, its tip moves with supersonic speed, and the compression wave in front of the tip is heard as a loud crack.

When an airplane is traveling at less than the speed of sound, it compresses the air in front of it. At 750 miles per hour, the nose waves of an airplane suddenly become sound waves. These waves cause the sonic boom, which often sounds like a heavy explosion in the sky.

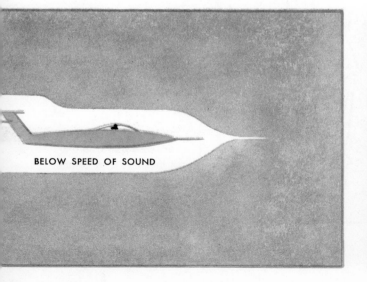

BELOW SPEED OF SOUND

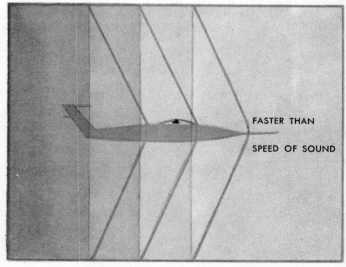

FASTER THAN

SPEED OF SOUND

Some Interesting Facts About Sound

You have learned enough about sound to answer the following questions. Try to answer them before you read the answers.

It is not unusual for soldiers marching in a long column to be out of step. This is likely to be true when soldiers are march-

Why are soldiers at the rear of a column sometimes out of step?

ing in time to the music of a band at the head of the column. Can you tell why the soldiers at the rear are out of step? We learned that it takes time for sound waves to travel through air. The music of the band reaches the soldiers at the rear of the column after it is heard by the soldiers leading the column. If the column is about 600 feet long, the soldiers at the rear will be a whole pace out of step with those who are leading.

Have you ever noticed that the horn of an approaching car seems to

Why does an approaching automobile horn have a higher pitch than usual?

have a pitch that is higher than usual. You probably noticed this most clearly just as the automobile reached you, for at that moment, the pitch of the horn suddenly dropped to a much lower note. As sound waves move outward from the horn, waves that are moving in the same direction as the automobile will reach anyone standing to the front of the automobile with the normal speed of sound — *plus* the speed of the vehicle. As a result, if you stand to the front of the automobile, more than the normal number of sound waves reach you per second. This has the same effect as increasing the frequency of the sound, because frequency is measured in waves

While marching to the beat of a band, soldiers at the rear of a column are often out of step. Can you explain why this happens?

(or cycles) per second. Now, we have learned that an increase in frequency results in an increase in pitch. Thus, the horn of an approaching automobile seems to increase in pitch.

At the moment the automobile passes

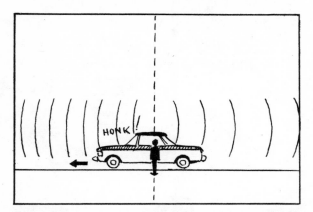

As a train moves away from you, fewer sound waves reach your ear per second than when the train approaches you. This causes the seeming drop in pitch as the train speeds by.

you, the sound waves now moving sidewise from the horn have only their usual speed. Thus, the frequency is lower and so is the pitch.

After the automobile has passed you, the sound waves reach you with the normal speed of sound — *minus* the speed of the automobile. Fewer sound waves reach you per second. This is the same as lessening the frequency — and consequently, lowering the pitch of the sound.

The seeming change in the pitch of a moving sound is called the *Doppler Effect*. The reason for the seeming change was first given by an Austrian physicist, Christian Johann Doppler, in 1842. While walking with his little daughter, he heard the seeming change in pitch of a train whistle, and this prompted him to think about the reason for it.

Why is it easier to hear sounds from a boat during the day than at nighttime?

On a sunny day, people at the beach are sometimes surprised to find how well they can hear sounds coming from boats not very far offshore. And at night, people in boats near the shore can hear sounds from land quite clearly. Why is this so? On a sunny day, the sun heats the surface of the land faster than the surface of water. The air over the land is warmed quickly and it rises. The place of this air is taken by cooler air flowing in from over the water. This air carries with it the sounds

At the beach, it is easier to hear sounds coming from a boat during the day than at night. But on a boat, it is easier to hear sounds coming from the beach at night than during the day.

that were made over the surface of the water — on boats, for instance.

At night, the surface of the water is warmer than the surface of the land. This reverses the flow of air, so that it goes from land to water. Thus, sounds on land are carried out to persons who are in boats.

47

You can hear the "sound of the sea" in a sea shell only when other sounds cause the shell to resonate.

When can you hear the "sound of the sea" in a shell? Once there was a man who found a large sea shell on the shore. He put it to his ear and heard what seemed to be the sound of the sea coming from the shell. He decided to take it home to his children. While he was driving home, he was stopped for a while in traffic. He put the sea shell to his ear and was pleased to hear the "sound of the sea" quite clearly.

When he reached home, he showed his children what he had found. Wanting them to hear the sounds in the shell as clearly as possible, he took his children into a quiet room. But when the children put the sea shell to their ears, they could hardly hear anything. What had happened?

When the man held the sea shell to his ear on the beach, the shell acted as a resonator for the sounds of the waves breaking in the surf. The noises of traffic, too, caused the shell to resonate and to produce a sighing sound of varying strength, much like the sound of the sea. In the quiet room, however, there was little continual sound to make the shell resonate.

Your new world of sound . . . You have learned much about sound. The many sounds that you hear all day long can take on a new meaning, now that you understand how and why they are made and act as they do. This scientific knowledge should increase your interest in the world of sound that is around you.

THE HOW AND WHY WONDER BOOK OF
ATOMIC ENERGY

Written by DONALD BARR
Assistant Dean, School of Engineering
Columbia University

Illustrated by GEORGE J. ZAFFO

Editorial Production: DONALD D. WOLF

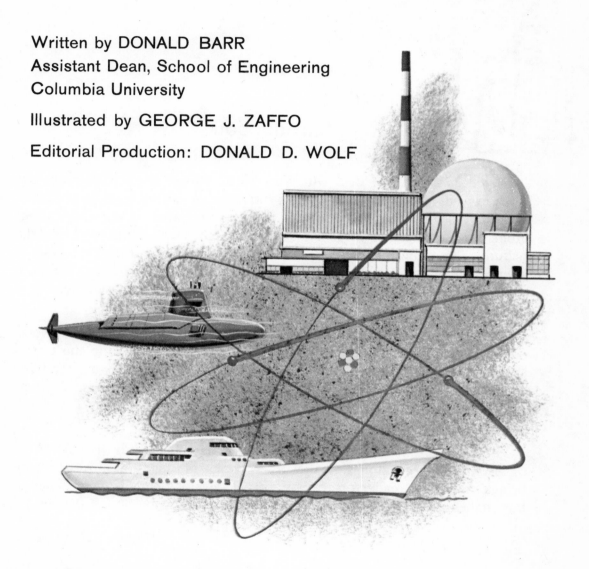

Edited under the supervision of
Dr. Paul E. Blackwood
Washington, D. C.

Text and illustrations approved by
Oakes A. White, Brooklyn Children's Museum, Brooklyn, New York

GROSSET & DUNLAP • **Publishers** • **NEW YORK**

Introduction

Big ideas sometimes deal with very small things, and small things are often exceedingly important. Witness the atom. Scientists have had some of their biggest ideas about these tiny particles of matter. Their ideas about atoms have changed as discoveries have brought new information into the picture. *The How and Why Wonder Book of Atomic Energy* takes the science-minded reader along the exciting road of discovery about the atom that led to the first use of atomic energy in a controlled way, and tells how people from many countries made scientific contributions.

The life-blood of scientific activity is in exploring all parts of the universe — even the tiny parts represented by atoms — and explaining the events that take place. Though individual atoms cannot be seen, they are the basis of all matter. And in the search for more information about atoms, scientists gradually came upon new knowledge about the energy within. This book tells this wonderful story.

Parents and schools will want to place *The How and Why Wonder Book of Atomic Energy* alongside the other books in this series. It not only brings the young reader up to date on the development of atomic energy, but challenges one to think about the yet-to-come atomic age of the future.

Paul E. Blackwood

Dr. Blackwood is a professional employee in the U. S. Office of Education. This book was edited by him in his private capacity and no official support or endorsement by the Office of Education is intended or should be inferred.

Library of Congress Catalog Card Number: 61-16047

Contents

An atomic bomb destroyed Hiroshima.

A B-29 bomber dropped the first wartime A-bomb.

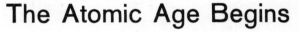

The Atomic Age Begins

At 8:15 in the morning, on August 6, 1945, people in the Japanese city of Hiroshima were getting out of bed, eating breakfast, beginning the day's work. Japan was at war. Nazi Germany's terrible clanking armies had been beaten, and the madman Hitler who had murdered whole countries was dead. The dictator Mussolini was dead, too, and Italy had gone over to the other side. The Japanese empire, which had started out to conquer the whole world with those partners, was now left to face the United States and her allies alone. General MacArthur's armies were already shooting and slashing their way into the islands that guarded Japan. For weeks American planes had rained fire bombs on Japanese cities. Thus far, Hiroshima had been spared. Then a lone American plane streaked over the city. It dropped one bomb. The Atomic Age had begun.

DEATH OF A CITY

There was a vast flash of fire, brighter than the sun, and hotter. There was a great shuddering of the earth and a great roar and a scorching wind. There was a cloud shaped like a huge mushroom, silently standing above the ruins. There was nothing left of the center of Hiroshima except charred, dusty rubbish from which deadly invisible rays were streaming. There were 78,150 people known to be dead and 13,983 people missing. From one bomb!

The President of the United States, Harry S. Truman, broadcast a warning to Japan. This, he said, was a new kind of bomb, a bomb which used the forces that made the sun hot, and America had more of these bombs. The President was slightly wrong in his science. But that did not matter. The Japanese knew that there *was* a new force in the world, and soon they surrendered.

On that August day, in laboratories all over the United States, scientists shivered and looked grim. That was not the way they had wanted the Atomic Age to begin.

The first atomic explosion on earth occurred in the New Mexico desert near Alamogordo in July, 1945.

Dawn in the Desert

Let us go back three weeks. It is a little before 3:00 o'clock in the morning on July 16, 1945. The rain is pouring down and the lightning is wildly stabbing the clouds over a lonely corner of Alamogordo Air Base in the New Mexico desert. It is not deserted tonight.

Men are scurrying through the darkness. There are soldiers, some of them wearing generals' stars. There are quiet men in business suits, whom the others address respectfully as "Professor." Between the crashes of thunder, they talk in little groups nervously. They go into a shed to examine some wires and instruments and drive away. Some go to another blockhouse a few miles away. Some drive six miles through the storm

and climb a tall steel tower to peer at a bulky, strange device nestling there among more wires and instruments. This is the device which is to be tested — an atomic device. It is known simply as "Fat Man." The men keep looking at the sky.

ZERO HOUR

At 3:30 there is a decision. Fat Man will be tested. At 4:00 o'clock the rain stops, but the clouds are thick overhead. By 5:10, the men have all gathered in the blockhouses. A voice crackles from the loudspeakers: "Zero minus twenty minutes." Men are rubbing suntan lotion on their faces and arms. The talking dies down. Some of the men are

praying. In one shed, when zero minus two is called, everyone lies on the floor, face down, with his feet pointing to the tower several miles away. In the other shed, the civilian scientist in charge of the project, Dr. J. Robert Oppenheimer, is hardly breathing. He holds onto a post to steady himself. At zero minus forty-five seconds, the automatic timers click on. The red hand glides around the clock face. Then the announcer yells, "Now!"

A blazing flash from the tower lights up the face of the desert and the mountains around it. There is an earsplitting roar which goes on and on. A blast of air knocks down two men who have stayed outside one of the sheds. An enormous, many-colored cloud boils up and up until it is eight miles tall. As it rises, the storm-clouds seem to move aside for it.

In the two sheds, the stiff faces have eased into smiles. Everyone is shaking everyone else's hand. There are shouts of laughter. A distinguished chemistry professor from Massachusetts throws his arms around Dr. Oppenheimer. "We did it! We did it!"

Fat Man has passed the test. The first atomic explosion on earth has just taken place.

A Dangerous Game

Let us go back two and a half years. It is mid-morning in Chicago, December 2, 1942. For a long time the University of Chicago has not played any football in its stadium, Stagg Field. It is a pity to waste the place. Under the grandstands there are rooms and courts for playing other games, and something is certainly going on in a squash court under the West Stands. But this is not squash, which is played with a rubber ball and rackets. This game is played with balls and rackets too small to see — hundreds of millions of them. The players can get hurt.

Above one end of the court is a balcony. Toward the other end, there is a monstrous black pile of something. It is strange-looking stuff, yet it somehow seems familiar. It is not metal, yet it is shiny, even a little greasy-looking. Where have we seen it before? In a pencil.

The "lead" in a pencil is not lead at all, but a form of carbon called *graphite*. Carbon comes in many forms, including coal and diamonds, but graphite is best for playing the atomic game. It can be sawed into neat shapes like wood. It can be made very pure. It is not rare.

FIFTY-TWO TONS OF URANIUM

This pile is made of neatly sawed bricks, stacked crisscross. It is very pure — or the players in the squash court hope it is — because if it isn't, something might go terribly wrong. And there are 1,350 tons of graphite in the court, piled 30 feet wide, 32 feet long, 21½ feet high. Some of the bricks in the middle of the stack have holes drilled in them. In these holes are lumps of a strange, rare metal called *uranium*. Almost all the uranium metal in the United States of America — fifty-two

tons of it — is here, buried in the big black pile under the seats at the football field. Also buried in the pile are 14,500 lumps of other stuff that has uranium in it.

Other holes have been drilled through the stacked graphite bricks. Lying in these are long rods of another rare metal, called *cadmium*. What the strange uranium can do, the strange cadmium can stop — the players hope.

For this game has never been played before, not since the creation of the earth. As the cadmium rods are pulled out of the pile, millions of tiny "balls" — much too small to see, even with a microscope — will shoot out of the uranium lumps. They will go right through the graphite and hit nearby uranium lumps, knocking more tiny balls out of them. These, too, will begin flying around and knocking more balls into the game. And the uranium and graphite will get hotter and hotter and hotter, like a furnace.

WILL IT WORK?

Now if the players are wrong, either of two things might happen. One is — nothing. There may not be enough balls, or they may not shoot through the graphite. Three years of hard work and millions and millions of dollars would be wasted. The other thing that might happen is — an explosion. There may be too many balls. The "furnace" may get too hot. And if it does, it could blow up not only the players and the squash court and the football field, but Chicago, Illinois.

8

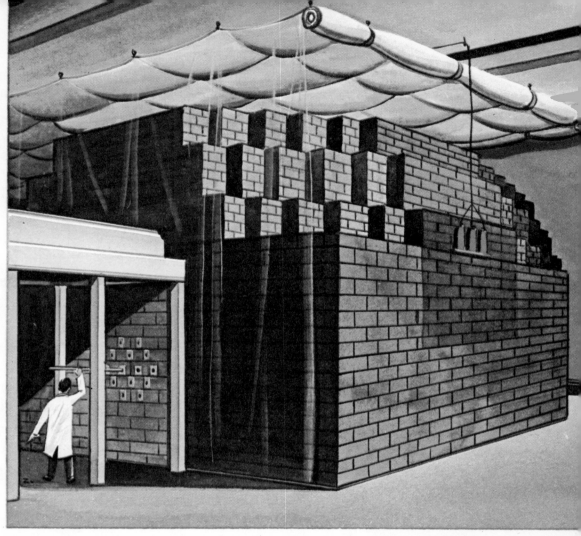

The first atomic reactor, at Stagg Field in Chicago, Illinois, was a huge stack of carbon bricks. The central bricks had holes with lumps of uranium in them. Other holes were drilled through the stack for the cadmium "control rods," shown in diagram below.

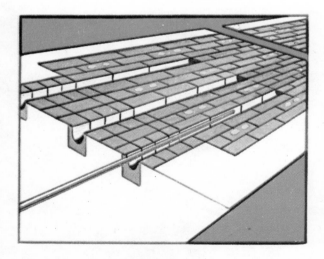

Now the players are ready. The captain of the team is an Italian-born scientist named Enrico Fermi. He invented the game. He has come from Columbia University in New York, a thousand miles away, to play. One of the players has his hand on a cadmium rod, waiting for the captain's signal to start the game. Three players are standing on top of the pile with big pails of water in their hands. The water has cadmium in it. If the game gets too "hot," they will douse it with the cadmium water before it blows up — *if* they have time. The scorekeeper is sitting at a cabinet covered with dials, like the dashboard of a car multiplied by ten. The dials tell him how many balls are flying, how hot the pile is getting. He will try to cry out a warning if the game goes wrong.

Fermi is sure it will not go wrong, and he is a world-famous physicist. He has checked his plans and calculations over and over again. He has checked them this morning. He does not think he will be like Mrs. Murphy's cow, which kicked over a lantern and started the Great Chicago Fire.

THE GAME STARTS

He gives the signal. A cadmium rod is pulled out. Another. All but one. The scorekeeper reports that the game is under way inside the great black heap.

The player takes the last cadmium rod and slowly pulls it out one foot. The scorekeeper's instruments click out the news — the pile is warming. It steadies, as Fermi's calculations said it would, before it gets really hot. The player pulls the rod out a little more. Then a pause. Check the instruments. Check the calculations. A little more. Check. A little more. Inch by inch.

It is lunchtime. Professor Fermi and his team go out to eat. After lunch, they inch the last cadmium rod out of the pile. At 3:25 P.M. the instruments have news. The pile has "gone critical" — it is hot — it is working.

Will it go too far, get too hot, explode? The clocks tick away the minutes. Still safe. At 3:53 P.M., Fermi tells the player with the rods to put them back. The game is over.

It is won. Man has built an atomic furnace. It can make electricity to light houses and run factories. It can make medicine to cure diseases. And it can make terrible explosives capable of killing thousands of people in a second.

One of the players reaches into his

Science has learned to use the energy of the atom for homes, factories, submarines, surface ships and medicine.

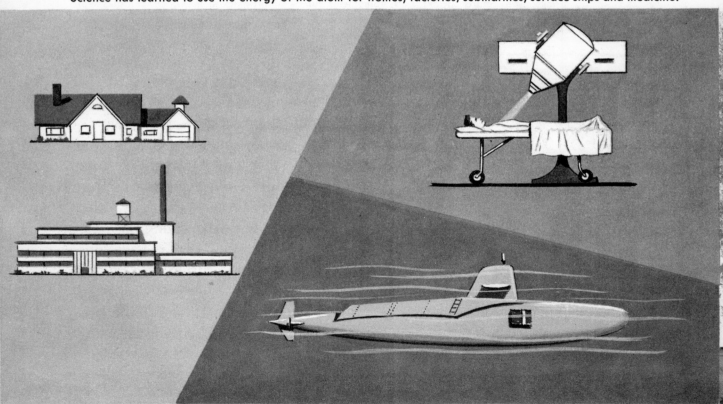

luggage and pulls out a bottle of Italian red wine. Fermi sends for paper cups. The members of the team hold their cups up — "Here's to the Atomic Age!"

A Little Extra Work

Let us go back four years. It is the evening of January 25, 1939, a cold, blowy evening in New York City. In a small, messy room in a basement at Columbia University, three men are working late.

For young Professor Dunning, it has been a busy day, and there is a lot more to do. He had lunch today with his friend Professor Fermi, who told him some exciting news. The news came in

Atomic power can also be used destructively.

a roundabout way, from Berlin, Germany.

Things are bad in Berlin. The madman Hitler is running Germany and Austria, and he is having thousands of people beaten or shot because he doesn't like their religion or their political beliefs or because they oppose the inhuman methods of the Nazis. Many Germans and Austrians are escaping to other countries. One Austrian woman, Dr. Lise Meitner, who is now in Denmark, is an important physicist.

LETTER FROM BERLIN

A few weeks ago she got a letter from Otto Hahn, a chemist who has stayed in Germany. He said he had been experimenting with some uranium and discovered a strange thing — some of it had turned into another metal entirely. He hardly dared think what that meant. As soon as she read this, Dr. Meitner saw what it meant. She talked it over with friends in Denmark. One was Niels Bohr, who is the world's greatest expert on atoms. And Bohr was just leaving for a visit to America.

A few days ago he arrived and told some American scientists he was going to give a report on this new discovery to a meeting in Washington, tomorrow, January 26. The news has been spreading fast. Fermi talked it over with Dunning at lunch today, and then left for Washington to attend the meeting.

Young John Dunning, too, sees what it means. He sees that if you really do to uranium what Otto Hahn says he did to uranium, little bits of stuff will shoot out of it — little balls too small to see, even with a microscope. And there will be sparks or flashes of energy — too small to see or feel. So all afternoon he has been trying to get equipment set up for a wonderful experiment. He is going to do what the German chemist did, and he is going to prove that the little bits of stuff really do fly off, and he is going to measure the energy. . . .

A SOUND NOBODY EVER HEARD

Dunning has clever hands. He has a way with gadgets. Here are some chunks of lead like children's blocks, and some chemicals and pipe and a lot of wire and some radio tubes and a

The oscilloscope recorded the sparks of energy from uranium atoms Dunning smashed.

small metal case with a round glass screen in one end. This is the equipment. It looks pretty sloppy, but it will work. It will do three things. It will

change the uranium. It will detect any flying bits of stuff or sparks of energy. And each time anything is detected, it will send an electric current into the thing that looks like a toy television set.

Two scientists who are working with him have come. Everything is ready. Dunning turns a switch on the case with the window. A glowing green line appears across it. He switches on the rest of the equipment. The green line becomes wiggly, almost furry. And then it happens.

A long green streak shoots up from the furry line. Blip! The signal. A second later, another. Blip! Blip-blip! Blip! Blip-blip-blip . . .

The three men are looking at atomic energy.

A Very Strange Idea

The whole universe — the great flaming stars scattered over billions of billions of miles, the earth under our feet, the air we breathe, the light we see by, the mysterious tiny blood cells flowing through our veins — all of this is made of only two kinds of things. One is *matter*. The other is *energy*.

What is the universe made of?

Intelligent men have been living on the earth for 100,000 years. But it is only sixty years ago that they began to find out what matter and energy really are. We still have a great deal to learn.

Have you ever had this experience? You stare at a word on a page, an ordinary word you have read hundreds of times, and after you concentrate on it for a few minutes it begins to look a little bit "wrong." The longer you study the letters in it, the stranger it becomes, until you almost believe it is misspelled. (Try it for three minutes with the word ENERGY. . . . Now: is that a real word?) It is the same way with the science of physics. As we study the whole page of the universe, the complicated things become wonderfully simple. But when we concentrate on the simple words on the page of the universe, they become very complicated and unfamiliar.

What is the difference between matter and energy?

At first glance it looks as if matter and energy are quite different — matter weighs something and energy does not. However, since the year 1900, physicists have been giving this question a second, third and fourth glance. They have been puzzled by the fact that energy often acts like matter and matter acts like energy.

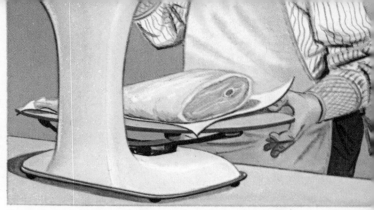

Mass is the amount of matter in a thing — meat, for example. One way to measure mass is with a scale.

But that's not always easy. The air above this scale has one ton of mass. Why doesn't what you see here take place?

Answer: Because the air also gets underneath the scale and pushes upward, just like water under a rowboat.

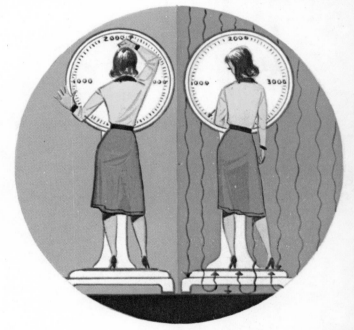

Another way to measure the mass of a thing is by the kind of wallop it gives when it hits you head-on.

FORE!

1 ERG = 1/10,000,000 JOULES
1 HORSEPOWER-HOUR = 198,000,000 FOOT-POUNDS
1 BRITISH THERMAL UNIT = .0002930 KILOWATT-HOURS
1 LARGE CALORIE = 2,087 FOOT-POUNDS

To the physicist, the word "work" means anything that uses energy — whether it's electricity, sunlight, chemical energy in food or rocket fuel, muscle exercise. Even watching T.V. or sunbathing takes work.

1 LARGE CALORIE = 2,087 FOOT-POUNDS
1 ERG = 1/10,000,000 JOULES

The paper this book is printed on is matter, and it seems fairly solid and not particularly strange. It weighs something in your hand. Blow against it. It moves a little. Blow harder. It moves more. It has what physicists call *mass*.

The breath you blow against the book is not solid like the book, and at the moment you cannot tell that it weighs anything. There are several hundred miles of air piled on top of you, and yet you are not crushed. But a second's thought tells you that, although the matter in your breath is much more loosely arranged than the matter in the book, it has body to it, for when you blow up a balloon, you can feel the air

1 HORSEPOWER-HOUR =
198,000,000 FOOT-POUNDS
1 BRITISH THERMAL UNIT =
.0002930 KILOWATT-HOURS

1 ERG = 1/10,000,000 JOULES
1 HORSEPOWER-HOUR =
198,000,000 FOOT-POUNDS
1 BRITISH THERMAL UNIT =
.0002930 KILOWATT-HOURS

inside. And air actually weighs quite a lot. For a blimp, carrying crew and engines and fuel, floats in the sky by weighing a little less than air, just as a submarine floats in the sea by weighing a little less than water. So even very thinned-out matter has mass.

How can we tell matter from energy?

But the light by which you are reading this book is something else. It does not seem to weigh anything. You can shine a flashlight beam into a balloon and the balloon will not fill. If you blow sideways against the beam, it will not shift. Light does not seem to have any mass. It is not thinned-out matter, but energy.

Yet, when we stare at matter very hard and long, using the marvelous electronic and magnetic eyes that science has invented, it begins to look very strange. It does look almost like a queer kind of thickened-up or frozen energy.

What is energy?

We still do not know very clearly what energy is. But we know what it does. It does *work*. Technically, we say that work is the applying of a force over a distance. More simply, it is the use of energy to move things or to change things. Work may be moving pieces of matter around — lifting a girder up the skeleton of a skyscraper, drilling a hole in the earth, hammering a nail, weaving cloth. Work may be changing the insides of matter — refining iron ore into iron metal, changing iron to steel in an open-hearth furnace, using derivatives of coal, air and water to make material called nylon. Work may be magnetizing and demagnetizing something, as happens thou-

Energy is stored in matter. Coal is black and cold, but it stores light and heat from the sunlight of over three hundred million years ago.

Prehistoric ferns grew in large numbers, using the sunlight to build up plant fibers from the simple chemicals of the air and water.

Drowned in swamps and shifting oceans, crushed under huge layers of rock, the leaves and stems of the plants turned hard and black, but they did not change back to the original chemicals.

When you burn coal, the fossils of plants turn back to chemicals, something like the ones from which they were made, and the ancient sunlight is released — as fire.

sands of times a second in a loud-speaker. Work may be changing the temperature of something.

We measure energy by the amount of

How do we measure energy?

work it does. We measure it in *foot-pounds*. For example, 20 foot-pounds is the amount of energy it would take to lift 2 pounds 10 feet, or 10 pounds 2 feet, or 5 pounds 4 feet. We also measure energy in *calories*. A "small calorie," the kind people count when they are dieting, is a thousand times bigger — so a man on a strict diet might eat only enough food to give him 3,000,000 foot-pounds of energy a day. We also measure energy in *joules, ergs, horsepower-hours, kilowatt-hours,* and all sorts of units, depending on the kind of work we mean.

In the year 1900, every physicist in the

Can we "make" energy?

world would have told you that we cannot make new energy — we can only use energy which exists already. Of course we can make electrical

energy, but we make it out of other energy, energy in another form.

Energy exists in many forms, and we have learned how to change it from form to form. Suppose you build a fire. It gives you *heat-energy*. With that you could boil water and use the steam to push the piston of the steam engine, which would turn a wheel, giving you *mechanical energy*. That might in turn drive a dynamo, changing the mechanical energy into *electrical energy*. That electricity could work a lamp, which would turn it into *light-energy*. Or a stove, which would change it back to heat-energy. Or a motor, which would change it back to mechanical energy.

In doing all this, said the scientists of 1900, you have not added any energy to the universe. You took some energy which had been stored up in matter — just as mechanical energy is stored in a wound-up watchspring — and *converted* that energy until it had done the work you wanted.

They were nearly right, which in science, where there is no "nearly," means that they were wrong.

Energy can be changed to other forms. Fire (heat energy) boils water. Steam drives an engine which turns a wheel (mechanical energy), which drives a dynamo (electrical energy), which lights a lamp (light energy).

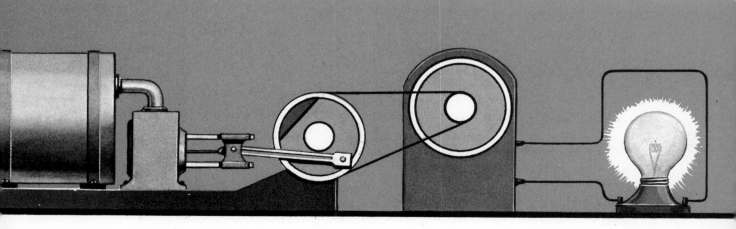

The scientists of 1900 were also sure we could never destroy any energy. We could only lose it.

Energy is always leaking away and taking forms in which we cannot catch it and use it. The fire under your boiler heats other things besides the wa-

Do we burn up energy?

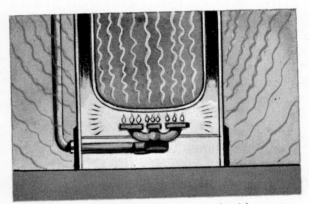

Fire under a boiler heats other things besides water.

ter in the boiler. The steam seeps out around the piston. The air around the hot cylinder of the steam engine warms up and blows away. The dynamo heats up from friction, and this energy is also carried away by the air. Your electric wires get warm. The light bulb gives off heat as well as light, and that, too, is carried away. So as you go on converting energy from one form to another, you are, so to speak, cooking the wind. At last, this escaped energy radiates off, like the sun's rays, into the endless cold of outer space.

But it still exists somewhere out there. It is not destroyed. The human race sends about 90,-000,000,000,000,000,000 foot-pounds

Where does used energy go to?

of energy out into space each year. So in 1900, physicists had the idea that we can never change the amount of energy in the universe, and they were so sure of this that they called it a scientific law — the *Law of the Conservation of Energy*. Now we know it is only half a law.

Suppose you were to hold a lighted match to the corner of a stack of paper. The paper would catch fire and the bright hot flames would eat across the sheets until the paper was burned up Some heat-energy and some light-energy would be given off, while one half an ounce of solid matter would seem to vanish. A bit of fluffy ash and a floating cloud of smoke would apparently be all that was left.

What happens when we burn matter?

Wouldn't you have changed that matter into energy then? Doesn't that mean matter and energy are really forms of the same thing after all?

In 1900, you could not have found a single physicist who would have answered "yes" to those questions. Now you could not find a physicist who would answer with a straight "no." This is the most important change of mind in human history. It is changing our lives — and maybe our deaths.

Can we change matter into energy?

So we should think carefully about such an experiment with a stack of paper. To burn it scientifically you would have to burn it inside a can. You would have to use a big can, so as to hold all

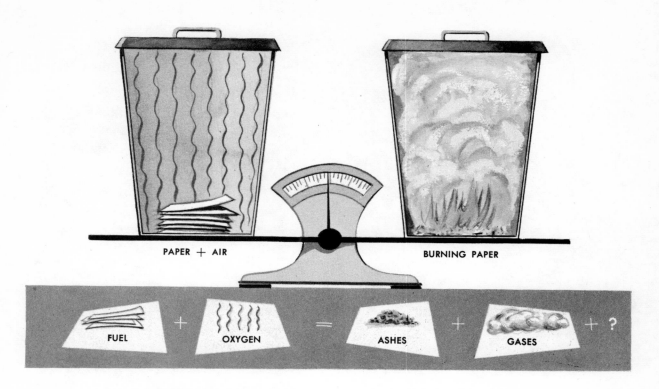

PAPER + AIR · BURNING PAPER

FUEL + OXYGEN = ASHES + GASES + ?

the air you needed for the fire. You would have to seal it up tight, so that absolutely no matter could get in or out. You would have to place the can on a scale while the paper burned and the can cooled off. And your scale would not show any change in weight.

In 1900, we all would have agreed that the ash and smoke and gases from the flame weighed *exactly* what the paper and air weighed to begin with. For we all thought then that there was another law of nature, called the *Law of the Conservation of Mass,* which said that no matter is ever added to the universe or taken away from it. Well, we know now that there actually *would* be a tiny loss of weight in that can. You could not have converted one half an ounce of matter into energy. But you would have converted one ten-billionth of an ounce of matter into energy. No scale in the world is good enough to

show it. But you would have done it. How do we know?

In the year 1905, a young German-born **When did physicists change their mind?** scientist was working in the Swiss Patent Office, checking other people's inventions. And he wrote a paper about what he called his *Theory of Relativity*. He hoped it would explain some facts about light and about the stars which had been mystifying physicists and astronomers for years. It did. It did something else, too. In this paper, Albert Einstein, one of the great scientific minds of all time, wrote a sentence which has become the most famous sentence of the twentieth century. Einstein did not write his sentence in words. He wrote it in algebra, the language of mathematics that uses letters of the alphabet to stand for numbers: $E = mc^2$.

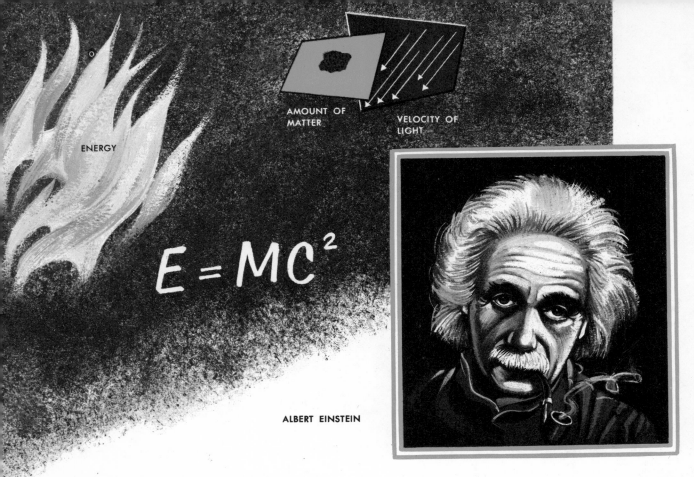

ENERGY

$$E = MC^2$$

AMOUNT OF MATTER

VELOCITY OF LIGHT

ALBERT EINSTEIN

We read this statement as "E equals m times c squared." It says

What does E = mc² mean?

that if you take a certain amount of matter and convert it into energy, you can calculate the number of foot-pounds you will get (which we have written down as E, for energy) by multiplying the number of pounds of matter you wipe out (which we have written down as m, for mass) by a certain number that is always the same (which we have written as c²). Or, if you change energy into matter, the same formula will tell you how much mass you get in exchange for your energy.

Einstein did not just say that this is what *would* happen if it *could* happen. He said it *does* happen. All the physicists had known that energy can be stored in matter and gotten out again, but they believed that this did not change the amount of matter. Einstein's brilliant theory said that when energy is stored in matter, it takes the form of a little additional mass, and when the energy is released, the mass goes back to what it was. In other words, instead of a Law of the Conservation of Energy and a separate Law of the Conservation of Mass, we now had one law, the *Law of Conservation of Mass-and-Energy*.

And this suggested a very strange idea. It was not some

Does E = mc² work for all kinds of matter?

particular little bits of energy or mass that might change back and forth. If only we know how, we could change *any* mass into energy.

No one did much about it for many years. In the first place, no one knew where to start. In the second place, scientists felt happy enough just having a tidy new theory which helped them calculate things they could not measure with instruments and which explained various odd facts they had never understood before. Most of them paid no attention to one letter in the famous equation. That was the letter c.

Now, in Einstein's theory, c stands for **How much energy can we get from matter?** speed of light. Light travels at 186,000 miles per second. The expression c^2 ("c squared") means the speed of light *multiplied by itself*. It gives us a gigantic number, 34,596,-000,000. If we do the arithmetic using this number, we find that from very little mass we get an astonishing amount of energy. When we burn a pound of coal in the ordinary way, we might get 10 million foot-pounds of energy. This is good. But if we could convert the whole pound of mass into energy, then by Einstein's formula we would get 30 million billion foot-pounds of energy. This is better.

If only we know how. . .

Inside the Atom

The ancient Greek philosophers wondered what would happen **What is matter made of?** if we took some solid matter — like stone or metal — and kept grinding it up into finer and finer powder. Some said that no matter how tiny the particles became, it would always be possible to break them up into still smaller particles by grinding harder. They believed that matter was made of a stuff called *hyle* (which is Greek for "stuff"), and that this was smooth right through and could be divided up endlessly.

Others said that no matter how hard or long we ground, we could not get the particles smaller than a certain size. They believed matter was made of separate hard lumps called *atoms* (which is Greek for "can't be cut"); and that these were the smallest things or particles there were.

Some ancient Greeks said matter could be ground endlessly. Others said atoms were the smallest things.

The second group was nearer to the truth, of course. Matter usually does consist of atoms. But they were wrong in thinking there was nothing smaller than an atom. And they certainly picked the wrong name for their fundamental particle. The atom can be cut.

For 2,200 years, no one had anything new or important to say

What are elements?

on the subject. Then in 1803, an English schoolteacher named John Dalton began to study atoms seriously. He figured out that some things are made up of only one kind of atom. These are pure *elements*. Gold and mercury and oxygen are elements. Other things are made of two, three or even more different kinds of atoms. These are *mixtures* and *compounds*. In mixtures the different elements are simply jumbled together. Air is a mixture of oxygen and nitrogen and other gases. In compounds, atoms of different kinds are actually linked together in little groups. Water is a compound in which each oxygen atom is linked up with two hydrogen atoms in a tiny package called a water *molecule*.

Dalton weighed and measured elements

What did Dalton discover about atoms?

and compounds until he began to find some rules for the ways in which the atoms could be linked and separated. He was able to calculate how much different atoms weighed compared to each other. But he still thought that atoms were little pellets—too small to see and too tough to cut, but not really different from grains of dust.

An atom — even an atom of iron in the

Are atoms solid?

steel armor-plate of a warship, or an atom of carbon in a diamond — is mostly empty space. The big old solid world around us is not solid at all. It is made of tiny spots of matter hanging or whirling quite far apart in open space.

Then why, if you pound your fist on the table, doesn't your hand go *into* the table-top? Because your hand, too, is empty space, and because strong electrical forces between the whirling spots hold them away from each other. Those forces, jostling the atoms in your flesh, are what you feel as the bang of your hand on the table.

We are sure of this although no one has ever actually seen an atom. Atoms are too small to see — 100 million of them in a row would take up less than an inch.

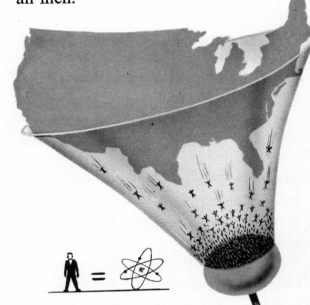

If people were no larger than an atom, the entire population of the U. S. could sit on the head of a pin, and there would still be space for several millions more.

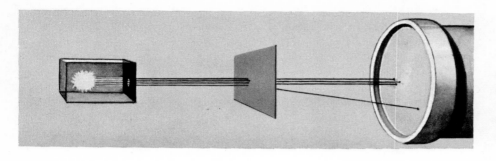

Most of the atomic bullets go through the "solid" metal — this shows that atoms are mostly empty space.

In 1911, an English physicist named Ernest Rutherford invented a way of testing whether atoms are solid. He shot them with even smaller particles. He got his "bullets" out of atoms of the element *radium*, which Pierre and Marie Curie of France had discovered and extracted from certain rocks. Radium atoms have a strange property. They are always breaking up little by little and flinging out tiny fragments of matter and little streams of energy. Several elements do this. They are called *radioactive* elements.

Can we see atoms?

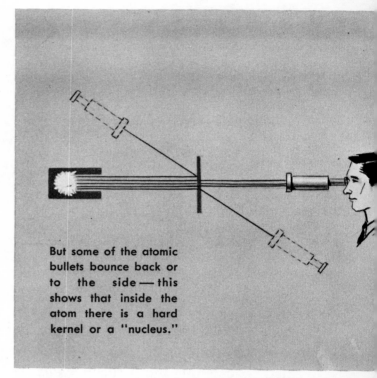

But some of the atomic bullets bounce back or to the side — this shows that inside the atom there is a hard kernel or a "nucleus."

Rutherford put some radium in a sort of gun-barrel made of lead. He aimed it at a target made of a fluorescent screen, like the front of a television picture tube. In between, he put a thin sheet of pure gold — but thin as it was, it was thousands of atoms thick, and shooting at it with the atomic "bullets" was like shooting with real bullets at armor-plate fifty feet thick. Yet the atomic bullets went through, and made little sparkles on the target screen.

How did we learn what is inside the atom?

And some of the sparkles were way off to the side, as if the atomic bullets had ricocheted. Rutherford realized what had happened. The bullets got

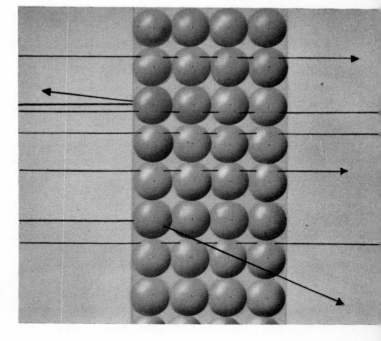

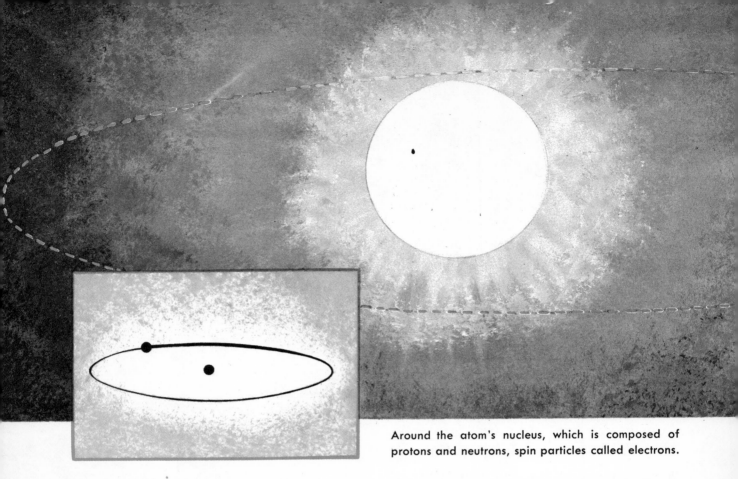

Around the atom's nucleus, which is composed of protons and neutrons, spin particles called electrons.

through easily because the gold atoms were not solid stuff, but open space. And in the middle of each atom there was a lump of mass, off which a bullet sometimes bounced. Rutherford decided to call this lump the *nucleus* of the atom, from the Latin name for the pit in a piece of fruit.

How do we look at atoms? Now we have hundreds of different devices for studying atoms, ranging from regular X-ray machines to fantastic jungles of wires and magnets and vacuum tubes called by such names as *cyclotron* and *bevatron*. One great *synchrotron* near New York City uses four thousand tons of magnets and a huge doughnut of metal a half mile around. With these huge machines, we can glimpse a little of what is going on in the tiny universe of the atom.

What is inside the atom? Scientists have put together all the facts they have gathered about the atom and they have a kind of picture of it in their minds. It looks something like a picture of our solar system. In the middle of the solar system the huge sun hangs in empty space. Around it, one inside the other, in paths or "orbits" like circles pulled out of shape, spin the planets, like our earth and Mars and Saturn.

In the middle of an atom, hanging in empty space, is the nucleus. Around it, in orbits like circles pulled out of shape, spin other tiny particles.

How big is the nucleus? The nucleus is so small it is hard even to think about how small it is. The atom itself is small—there are 6,000,000,000,000,000,000,000 atoms

24

The action of electrons spinning around the nucleus is much like the orbit of the earth around the sun.

sand and rock, down and down to the core of the world.

The nucleus is mostly made of two kinds of particles, *protons* and *neutrons*. The outer planet-particles are *electrons*. There are two kinds of electricity, which we call *positive* and *negative*. Two things that have positive electric charges push each other away. So do two things with negative charges. But if a positively charged thing and a negatively charged thing are near together, they pull at each other very strongly.

What is the nucleus made of?

in a drop of water. If you had that many strawberries, you could cover the whole world with a layer of strawberries seventy-five feet thick. And the nucleus takes up only $\frac{1}{1,000,000,000,000}$ of the space of the atom. If the nucleus were the size of a strawberry and you put it down in the middle of a big football field, right on the fifty-yard line, the outer "planets" of the atom would be going around in orbits way out over the spectators' heads, or even behind them.

But even though the nucleus takes up only a trillionth of the space in an atom, it has almost all the mass of the atom. Thus it is tremendously heavy for its size. A nucleus the size of a strawberry would weigh about 75 million tons. If you did put it down in the middle of a football field, the earth could not hold it. It would simply crush its way through

A nucleus that was the size of a strawberry would smash the earth's crust by its enormous weight.

The proton has a positive electric charge of a certain strength. The neutron has no electric charge at all. The electron, which is about 1,800 times lighter than the other two particles, has a negative electric charge — just as

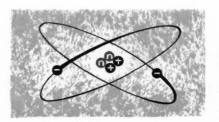

HELIUM ATOM

25

strong as the proton's, but the opposite kind. The nucleus or "sun" of the atom, therefore, has a positive charge. The outer electrons or "planets" have a negative charge. And the whole atom itself usually has no charge, because there are just as many protons in the nucleus as electrons whirling around it, so the charges balance or cancel each other. In the ordinary sodium atom, which is one of the atoms in salt, there are eleven protons and twelve neutrons in the nucleus, and eleven electrons going around in orbit.

By now, you will have thought of two questions. One is easy and one is hard.

The pull of the nucleus keeps the electrons in orbit just as your arm keeps the weight in its orbit, too.

If things with opposite charges attract each other, why doesn't the positive nucleus pull the negative electrons right down into it and just collapse the atom? Easy. The speed of

Why do the electrons keep flying around the nucleus?

the electrons makes them keep trying to fly off, away from the nucleus. Tie a weight to a string and whirl it around fast. You can feel the pull of the weight trying to fly away from your hand at the center. You have to pull a little to keep the weight in orbit. The electrical pull of the nucleus keeps the electrons in their paths, just as the pull of the sun's gravity keeps the earth in its orbit.

And if things with the same charges push each other away, why don't the protons in the nucleus just go flying off from each other in all directions? That one is hard. That is where atomic energy comes in.

By the way, if we were going to be very careful about words, most energy really could be called *atomic energy*. Because, as Einstein showed us, when energy flows around the universe it is always changing the mass of atoms. But when we think about the insides of the atom, we can see that there are two sorts of energy. One has to do with the outer electrons. The other has to do with the nucleus.

Is atomic energy a special kind of energy?

When two different atoms are linked together in a chemical compound, the nucleus of one does not join the nucleus of the other. Instead, some of the outer electrons change their orbits. Sometimes the two nuclei will share a few of these electrons. When a carbon atom forms the gas called methane, for instance, it shares electrons with four hydrogen

How do atoms form chemicals?

atoms. Or sometimes one nucleus steals an electron from the other by a complicated magnetic trick, and this leaves the thief-atom negatively charged and the victim-atom positively charged, so they stick together. This is how sodium and chlorine combine to make ordinary salt. It is as if the poor sodium atom kept following the chlorine atom around in the hope of getting its electron back. This kind of linking is called a *chemical* bond.

Sometimes when you make or break a **What is chemical energy?** chemical link, energy is given out, and this is called *chemical energy*. When an atom of carbon in a chunk of coal links up with two atoms of oxygen from the air, a compound called carbon dioxide — a gas with no color or smell — is formed, and at the same time heat-energy and light-energy are released. In other words, you have a fire. But this does not disturb the carbon nucleus or the oxygen nuclei.

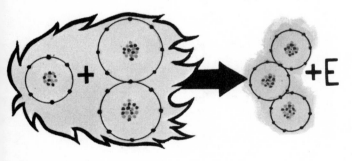

Heat given off when a carbon atom joins with two oxygen atoms is a simple form of chemical energy.

If you actually change the nucleus of an atom in order to get energy, you are doing something quite different. We ought to call this *nuclear energy*, but we usually just call it *atomic energy*.

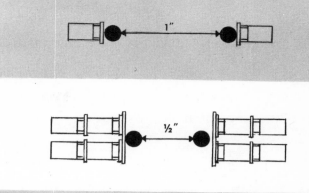

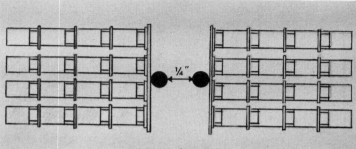

Things with the same electric charge push each other apart. When you divide the *distance* between them by 2, you multiply the *push* between them by 2 x 2.

We wish to turn matter into energy. **Where does "atomic energy" come from?** Well, then, we have to look at the place where practically all the mass in the universe is — the nucleus of the atom. We do not know much about the nucleus yet. One of the questions scientists are still wondering about is that hard question of yours: What holds it together?

Something must. We know how strong the forces are that push apart things that have the same electric charge. The closer together the two things are, the more powerful is the force that pushes them away from each other. If there is a certain push between them when they are 1 inch apart, there will be 4 times as much push when they are ½ inch apart, and 16 times at ¼ inch, and 64 times at ⅛ inch, and 256 as strong at ¹⁄₁₆ inch. At that rate, you can imagine how hard the push is between two protons rammed into a nucleus $\frac{1}{2,000,000,000,000}$ of an inch apart. It takes a lot of energy to keep them side by side.

This energy is called *binding energy*.

What holds the nucleus together? There is only one kind of atom that does not need any binding energy. That is the atom of hydrogen gas, which only has one proton in its nucleus. Some of the heavier kinds of atoms, with dozens of protons in their nuclei, have to have enormous amounts of binding energy. Where do they get it?

From mass. No one knows how a nucleus converts some of its own mass into energy in order to pull itself together. But physicists all agree that this is what happens. They can prove this by very carefully measuring the mass of an atom. Except for hydrogen, every atom weighs just a little bit less than it *ought* to.

Take helium gas, for instance. The helium nucleus

How much binding energy is in the nucleus? contains two protons and two neutrons. A proton by itself weighs 1.00758 of the tiny "mass units" that scientists have in-

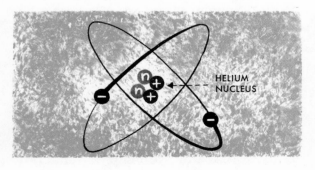

HELIUM NUCLEUS

vented for these measurements. A neutron weighs 1.00894. So the whole helium nucleus ought to weigh 4.03304. Instead, it weighs 4.00279. More than $\frac{3}{100}$ of a "mass unit" are missing. Using Einstein's $E = mc^2$ formula, we can calculate how much energy this is — what the scientists call 28 million "electron volts." This is only a tiny fraction of a foot-pound. But it is what keeps the universe from going *whoosh!* and turning into hydrogen. And it is what lets us turn matter into atomic energy.

There are hundreds of different kinds of

How many kinds of atoms are there? atoms in the universe. One way of sorting them out is to find out how many protons they have in the nucleus. All the atoms with one proton are *hydrogen* atoms. All with two are called *helium*. All with three, *lithium*. Four,

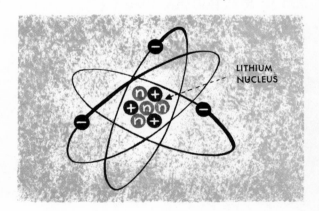

LITHIUM NUCLEUS

beryllium. Five, *boron*. Six, *carbon*. Seven, *nitrogen*. Eight, *oxygen*. And so on up to ninety-two, which is *uranium*. That is the heaviest kind of atom found in nature, though we have made a few heavier ones with our cyclotrons and atomic furnaces.

Each kind of atom with a certain number of protons is a different *element*. Until recently, we thought we were saying all we had to say about any atom if we just told what element it was. This, of course, is not so hard to do, because the number of protons in the nucleus is the same as the number of electrons out in orbit. These electrons are what make the atoms link chemically with other kinds of atoms or refuse to link with them. So clever chemists can always separate different elements.

Are all the atoms of an element the same? But there is another kind of particle in the nucleus — the neutron. Atoms with the same number of protons may come in different varieties, with different numbers of neutrons. Even the lightest and simplest element, hydrogen, comes in three varieties. The usual kind has one proton and no neutrons. Another, quite rare, has a proton and a neutron. It is sometimes called *deuterium,* but it is just "heavy" hydrogen. A third kind, called *tritium,* has to be made artificially. It has one proton and two neutrons, but it is still called hydrogen.

What is an isotope? Each of these varieties is called an *isotope*. The name was taken from the Greek words meaning "the same place," because isotopes of the same element always appear together in the chemists' lists. And that is more important than it sounds. Since different isotopes of the same element have the same number of outer electrons, they are just the same in chemical linkings and unlinkings, so that chemists have had a difficult time separating them. And since different isotopes of the same element behave quite differently when it comes to converting mass and releasing nuclear energy, they *must* be separated.

We have some wonderful machines that actually sort out atoms by weight. But they can only do it with a few atoms at a time.

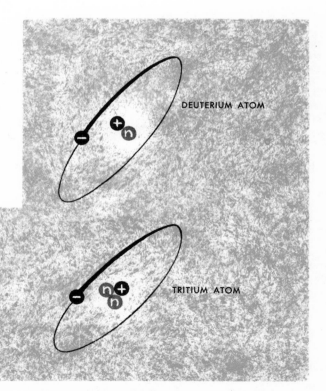

The usual hydrogen atom has 1 proton; deuterium has 1 proton, 1 neutron; tritium has 1 proton, 2 neutrons.

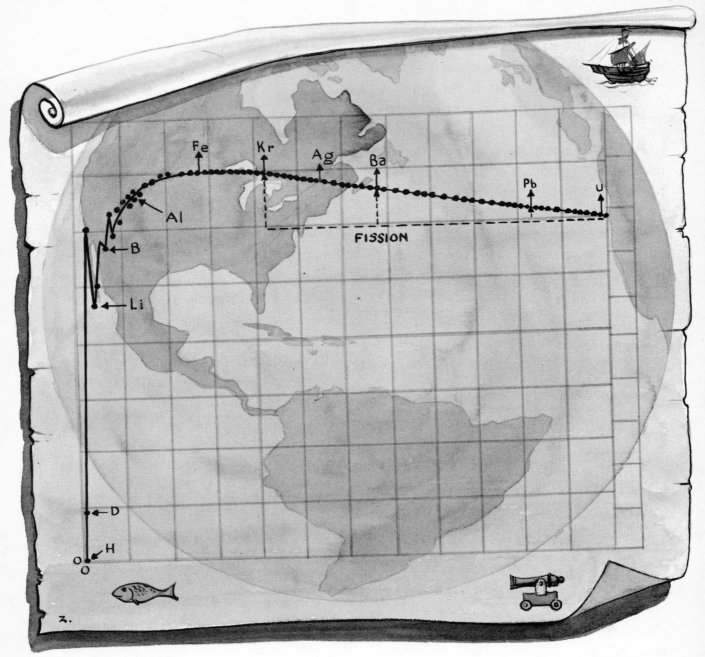

If you dig for buried treasure, the best thing you could possibly have is a map. The binding energy curve, a chart of all the isotopes in the world, tells us where we can dig energy treasure out of the nuclei of atoms.

This, however, is enough to give us the facts we need to make a great chart of isotopes called the *binding energy curve*. This chart tells us how much mass is "missing" from the nucleus of each of the hundreds of isotopes we have found or made. In other words, it

What is the "binding energy curve"?

tells us how much matter each kind of nucleus has mysteriously converted into energy to keep itself together.

This chart is why all the physicists were so excited when word spread that Hahn had turned the metal uranium into the metal barium. For the chart is like a map of buried treasure. It tells us where to dig for atomic energy.

It tells us that ordinary hydrogen has no mass missing. It tells us that helium, the next heavier element,

Did the big atoms have the most binding energy?

has quite a lot missing. As we go up through heavier and heavier kinds of atoms, we find more and more mass missing *for each particle in the nucleus* — up to a point. Up to a point — the element iron — and then, strangely enough, we find less and less mass missing for each particle in the heavier and heavier isotopes.

When we get to the heaviest element — the three isotopes of uranium — and look up how much mass is missing from the 234, or 235, or 238 nuclear particles — we find that much less of it has been turned into energy than in such middleweight elements as barium.

Think for a moment what this means.

It means that if we split up a uranium atom into two pieces, we will get

How can we get at some binding energy?

two smaller atoms — and something else. There are 92 protons in the uranium nucleus. Let us say the two pieces

happen to be not quite equal. One might have 36 protons in it — that would be the gas krypton. The other would have the remaining 56 protons — it would be barium. When you look at the chart you see that barium and krypton have *more mass missing* from them than uranium. So suddenly, some mass has disappeared from the universe.

And Einstein's formula tells us what has become of it. It has turned into energy — into the tremendous force with which the fragments of the uranium fly apart.

Maybe it is a little hard to see why this is energy we could use. Why doesn't

Why doesn't binding energy stay inside the atom?

this mass turn into energy that the nucleus uses inside of itself? As a matter of fact, it was hard for some physicists to be sure about this for a while. One answer is that binding energy does not work by brute force. It is something like the law that says you can't leave the country if you owe money to the government. The binding energy was energy that was given off when the protons and neutrons

Protons and neutrons owe energy to the nucleus and they are supposed to stay there until the debt is paid.

were packed together, and ordinarily they cannot get away unless this energy, this missing mass, is restored to the nucleus. But even if you can't leave legally, you could always *break* out. That is what happens when we split the atom.

And that is why the chart means this also: If we could mash a couple of hydrogen nuclei together so as to form a helium nucleus, we would also wipe out some matter. We would wipe out more matter, in fact, than by splitting uranium. The energy would be prodigious. It would be like making a sun. For this *is* how the sun gets its energy.

Atom Smashing

In 1896, before we knew anything about $E = mc^2$ or what the atom is like, a French physicist named Henri Becquerel had a slight accident in his laboratory. He was testing some uranium compounds for something and discovered that they gave off energy all by themselves. Soon after that Pierre and Marie Curie began to discover a whole group of new elements that did the same thing. Madame Curie named this strange behavior *radioactivity*.

Who discovered radioactivity?

For a long time, nobody was sure how radioactivity worked. Many experiments were done to find out just what these mysterious "rays" were. Some of them at last turned out to be helium atoms with their electrons knocked off. Some turned out to be fast-moving electrons. Some turned out to be real rays like very powerful X-rays. But what were they doing in those atoms? And why did they come out?

It slowly dawned on the scientists that what they were looking at were *atoms breaking down*. This was a rather frightening idea, for two reasons. In the first place, everyone at that time still thought atoms were unbreakable, everlasting little pellets. This showed they were not. And if pieces broke off an atom, what was left must be a different atom. That meant elements were changing into other elements. And if elements changed into other elements when particles flew out, then atoms probably were not the particles that "could not be cut" (as their name said), but were bundles of still smaller particles.

Do atoms ever split by themselves?

In the second place, the particles flew out with great energy and the rays were very energetic, too. These atoms seemed to be *making* energy, which everybody in

Why was radioactivity important?

The French physicist, Antoine Henri Becquerel (1852-1908), discovered natural radioactivity, the invisible radiation of uranium. With Pierre and Marie Curie, he won the Nobel Prize in physics for his great discovery.

The strange rays from uranium blackened a photographic film right through a light-proof cover, Becquerel found.

Pierre Curie of France (1859-1906) and his wife Marie (1867-1934) were the discoverers of radium in 1898. In addition to sharing the Nobel Prize with Becquerel and her husband in 1903, Marie Curie received the Nobel award again in 1911, in chemistry.

Let's pretend that you were very rich and that you had the very large sum of one million dollars, even after taxes.

And now let us also suppose that you have promised to give away half of all your money on every Friday of the week — even on Friday the thirteenth.

Then on the first Friday, you will give away $500,000. On the second Friday, you will give away $250,000 more. On the third Friday, $125,000 more.

Then we say that the "half-life" of your money is one week, because in one week, one half disappears.

But no matter how much you give, you will never go altogether broke.

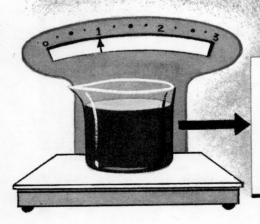

U-238 = 4,500,000,000 YEARS

RADIUM = 1,620 YEARS

FRANCIUM = 21 MINUTES

THORIUM = 14,000,000,000 YEARS

POLONIUM = 138 DAYS

NEPTUNIUM = 2½ DAYS

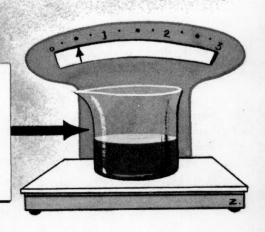

And — every radioactive isotope has its own "half-life."

those days *knew* was all wrong. When Einstein came along and said that this energy was converted from mass, it seemed like the best explanation.

So a lot of what we now know about atoms came from that laboratory accident.

Now all those radioactive atoms were quite heavy. It seemed that a heavy nucleus was not too sturdy. This suggested that if we could only smash up heavy atoms, instead of letting them decay slowly by themselves, we might change one element into another and perhaps even release energy much faster. But we had nothing with which to smash them.

The neutron is a quiet little particle.

Why are neutrons good atomic bullets? There are probably more neutrons in the universe than anything else, but it was not till 1930 that we found them — hiding right in the middle of everything. For years, physicists had been trying to make a picture of the atom that would explain the things atoms did. They tried all sorts of wild combinations of the positive proton and the negative electron. Then an Englishman named James Chadwick suggested, "Why not try drawing it with a particle a little bit bigger than the proton but without any electric charge?" Everyone realized this was the answer. And they realized that here, also, was the thing with which to smash heavy nuclei.

The problem is to hit the nucleus. Suppose you shoot at it with a positively charged proton. As it passes the negatively charged electrons, they will pull it to one side. As it approaches the posi-

tively charged nucleus, that will push it away. Suppose you shoot an electron. The positive nucleus will certainly pull the negative electron toward it. But electrons are too light. They cannot do enough damage. The neutron is heavy and it will not be pulled off its course.

So physicists set up various machines for using other particles to bounce neutrons out of the nuclei of light metals like beryllium. And they started shooting.

How do we split uranium atoms?

They kept shooting for seven years. All sorts of things happened. They made new elements, heavier than uranium. They made old elements radioactive.

And one day in January 1939, Otto Hahn found a little barium in the uranium that he had been bombarding with neutrons. The news spread that the uranium nucleus had been split, and young Dr. Dunning, remembering the binding energy chart, rushed up to his laboratory to measure the release of nuclear energy.

When a neutron hits a uranium nucleus, one of three things can happen. (1) It may bounce. That's that. (2) It may just stay there. Nothing would happen till later. So we will think about this. (3) It may break the nucleus apart.

What happens when a uranium atom splits?

Suppose a neutron hits a nucleus of one of the three ordinary isotopes of uranium. This is the isotope with 92 protons and 143 neutrons in it — called

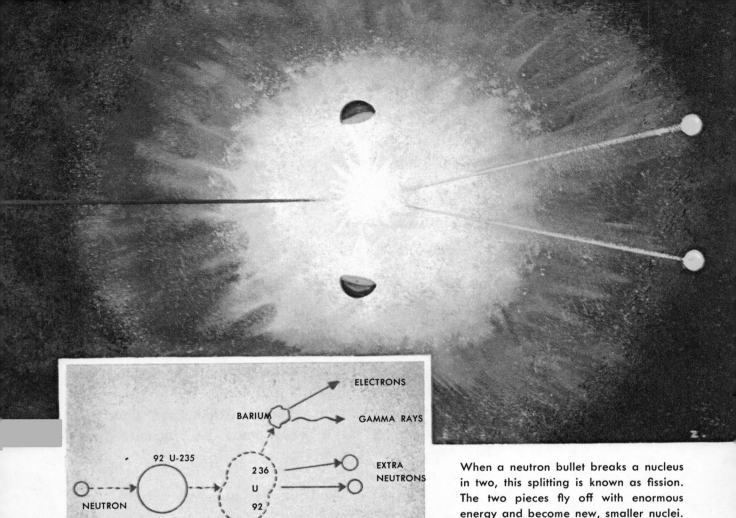

When a neutron bullet breaks a nucleus in two, this splitting is known as fission. The two pieces fly off with enormous energy and become new, smaller nuclei. Two new neutron bullets also shoot out.

U-235. The new neutron makes it U-236. But for some reason, U-236 never stays together. It bursts into pieces. There are many ways it can break. Suppose this time the biggest piece is a barium nucleus, with 56 protons and 88 neutrons. Another piece is krypton, with 36 protons and 54 neutrons. And there are at least two extra neutrons by themselves. *They* are *very* important. And there is a lot of energy, which makes all the pieces shoot off at terrific speeds.

This is called *fission*.

It is very nice to be able to smash atoms.

What is a "chain reaction"? But it is not a useful thing to do unless you get more energy out of it than you put into it. If you have to keep a building full of equipment pumping neutrons into uranium to split a few nuclei, you are just playing.

Think back for a moment to the paper-burning experiment. You touch a lighted match to the corner of one sheet. The paper catches fire. The flames spread. You do not have to set each

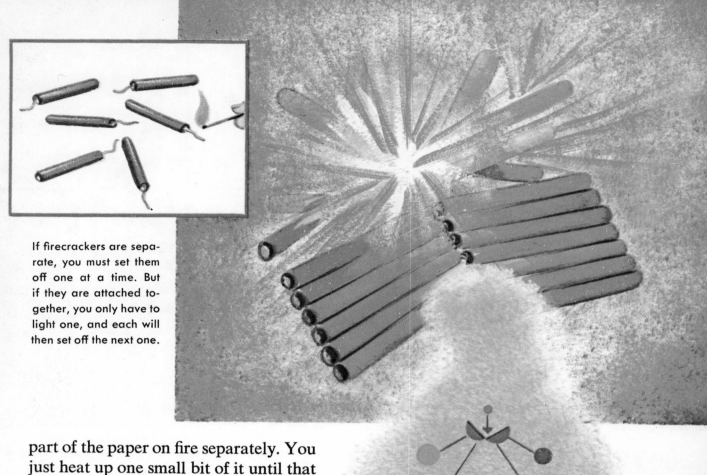

If firecrackers are separate, you must set them off one at a time. But if they are attached together, you only have to light one, and each will then set off the next one.

part of the paper on fire separately. You just heat up one small bit of it until that bursts into flame. The heat from that flame starts the next few fibers burning, and they light the next bit, and so on. This is called a *chain reaction.*

That is what we want to do with uranium. We need a chain reaction in which each bursting nucleus will shoot out neutrons that break up other nuclei near it. The two loose neutrons that fly out in the fission of a uranium nucleus give us atomic energy we can use.

But now suppose — as we again think of the experiment with the match and the paper — that the paper is damp. Each bit of paper would need so much heat to get it lit that the sections next to it would have burned away before it got started. The fire would go out.

What do we need to make a chain reaction?

A chain reaction is something like the firecrackers that are attached to each other. When a uranium atom splits, it shoots out neutron bullets that split nearby atoms, which split other atoms, and so forth.

In the same way, we need the right isotope of uranium for our atomic chain reaction. It has to have a nucleus that splits easily and that shoots out loose neutrons. The U-235 isotope is excel-

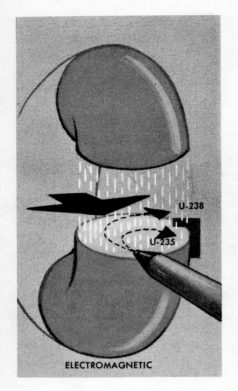

ELECTROMAGNETIC

U-238

U-235

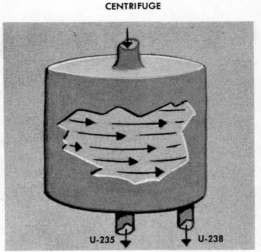

CENTRIFUGE

U-235   U-238

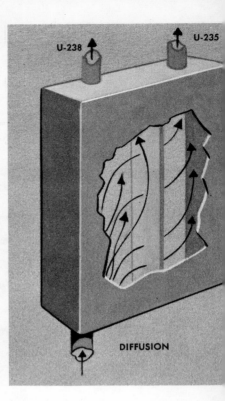

U-238   U-235

DIFFUSION

Scientists have figured out three ways to separate U-235 from U-238. In the electromagnetic way, the uranium is shot between the poles of a magnet, which separates the heavier atoms from the lighter ones. In the centrifuge way, the uranium is whirled around and the heavy atoms swing to the outside. In the diffusion way, more light atoms seep through the divider than heavy ones. Separation is necessary to make atomic fuel.

lent. But U-235 is hard to come by. No matter where natural uranium comes from — the Congo or Canada or Russia or in meteorites from outer space — it always contains the same amounts of its three isotopes. And less than a hundredth of it is U-235.

What isotopes are good atomic fuel? Another uranium isotope, U-234, only shows up in faint traces. We can hardly tell it is there. More than 99 per cent of uranium is the heavy isotope, U-238, with 92 protons and 146 neutrons. Unfortunately, it is like damp paper. The neutrons crash into the U-238 nucleus — and stay there. This is not bad. It has its uses. But it will not keep the atomic fire going.

Will other elements or isotopes work?

Yes — a man-made element called *plutonium* is excellent atomic fuel. Plutonium has 94 protons and 145 neutrons. We make it by putting U-238 in an atomic oven and "cooking" it in neutrons, so to speak. When a neutron hits the U-238 nucleus and stays there, it gives us a new uranium isotope with 92 protons and 147 neutrons. That is just too many neutrons, and this is a very shaky nucleus. But it does not break up. Instead it soon begins to break down. One of the neutrons mysteriously turns into a proton, and an electron — of all things — suddenly shoots out of the nucleus. Now we have a new element called *neptunium,* with 93 protons and 146 neutrons. But this nucleus is still rather rickety. Again a neutron changes into a proton and an electron pops out. Now we have plutonium.

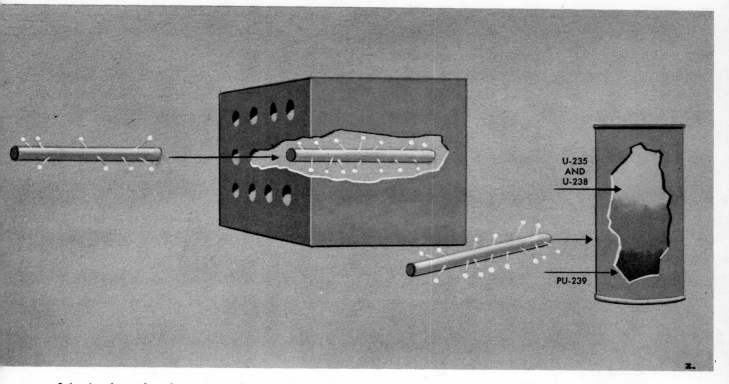

U-235
AND
U-238

PU-239

Z.

Scientists have found a way to change uranium-238 into the more useful atomic fuel plutonium. The U-238 is put into a reactor where it is bombarded with neutrons from U-235. Many of the U-238 atoms are built up into plutonium-239 atoms, which can be separated chemically. At one time, scientists thought that plutonium was an artificial element, but we now know that it occurs naturally and is found in the mineral pitchblende.

But in order to have it, we first have to

Can we make atomic fuel?

have a good atomic oven with plenty of neutrons. In other words, a chain reaction. In other words, U-235. That was the problem that nagged at American scientists in the years between 1939 and 1942.

Professor Fermi was sure he could build an atomic furnace that would work — and which could be used as an oven to cook up plutonium. Other scientists had calculated that if only they could get enough plutonium or enough U-235, they could make a bomb that would knock America's enemies right out of the war.

For during these years, Hitler's armies beat down nation after nation in Europe, and the Japanese struck without warning at Pearl Harbor and con-

quered hundreds of islands in the Pacific. Our scientists were afraid that the German scientists would make an atom bomb for Hitler, and that this cruel madman would rule the world.

Working day and night, chemists and physicists tried to invent a way of separating enough U-235 to start an atomic furnace.

One group said the way to do it was the

How do we separate isotopes?

way it was done in a mass spectrometer, by shooting electrically charged streams of uranium atoms between the poles of magnets. The government spent millions and millions of dollars to build *electromagnetic separators* at an out-of-the-way place in Tennessee called Oak Ridge. It was, and is, a good factory for separating isotopes, but it could not make enough U-235.

Another group said the way to do it was by *centrifugal force* — the force that makes things try to fly outward when they are whirled around in a circle. If we could make a gas or steam with uranium in it, and whirl it around in a tank, the compounds made with heaviest uranium atoms would go to the outside and we could pump them off. The Government had a factory built to try this, but it did not work well.

Professor Dunning and his Columbia group said the way to do it was to find a compound of uranium that was a gas, and put it in a tank with a porous wall — a wall with thousands and thousands of tiny holes in it — holes so small it would be hard for the gas to leak through. The particles of compound would be banging around

What is gaseous diffusion?

in the tank, and the ones made with heavier atoms would be moving more slowly than the lighter ones. So it would be the fast, light ones that would have the better chance of pushing through the porous wall — where they could be collected on the other side. Of course, some of the heavier particles would also get through, so we would have to do the filtering over and over again in tank after tank.

The gas that had to be used was a compound called *uranium hexafluoride*. It is a vicious stuff. It would eat right through ordinary tanks and pipes and pumps like a horrible acid. So for a long time, the Government held back. Then it told Professor Dunning to go ahead and design a huge factory to be built out of special materials at Oak Ridge. More millions of dollars were spent—and the *gaseous diffusion plant,* known in wartime code as K-25, worked.

(1) Mining it. (2) Milling it. (3) Refining it. (4) Separating U-235 from U-238 in a gaseous diffusion plant.

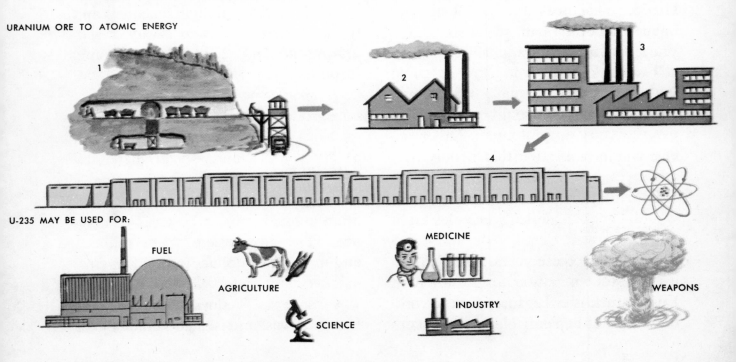

URANIUM ORE TO ATOMIC ENERGY

U-235 MAY BE USED FOR:

FUEL

AGRICULTURE

SCIENCE

MEDICINE

INDUSTRY

WEAPONS

At Bikini atoll in the Pacific, the U.S. set off an atom bomb under water. The cross section shows how an A-bomb works.

It is still working. It is an extraordinary place. Miles and miles of empty corridors lined with

What does an isotope separation-plant look like?

panels of dials and signal lights — miles and miles of tank rooms and pump rooms with no man to be seen — hundreds of miles of wires and automatic machinery — and every once in a while, a man will come down the hallway on a bicycle, copy a number from a dial, and ride back to the main control room. This is the place where America's atomic energy starts.

Once you have enough of the right iso-

How do we start the chain reaction?

tope, there is no trick at all to starting a chain reaction. You simply put enough of the isotope together in a lump and — off it goes!

How much is enough? It depends on the isotope. It depends on whether you are making a bomb or a furnace. It depends on how fast you let the neutrons travel. So you really have to calculate a different "enough" each time you use atomic energy. Some of these "enoughs" are still military secrets. This amount is called the *critical mass*. Because when you have it, you have a little crisis on your hands.

If you have less than the critical mass,

Why is there a "critical mass"?

the neutrons that come shooting out of your first split nucleus may be wasted. Since atoms are

41

mostly empty space, a neutron can go quite far, even through a heavy metal like uranium, before it bumps into a nucleus. And before it has a chance to do that, it might have shot right out of the lump. So if the lump is too small, so many neutrons are wasted that no chain reaction starts.

But if the lump is large enough, somewhere in it one of the billions and billions of atoms will split. It may split by itself, because uranium is radioactive. Or it may be split by one of the strange rays from outer space called *cosmic rays*. And when it splits, its neutrons will send the atomic blaze sweeping through the critical mass.

The simplest kind of atomic chain reaction is the one that **How does an A-bomb work?** takes place in a bomb. In the bomb are two or more lumps of isotope. Each lump weighs less than the critical mass, but together they weigh more than the critical mass. They are a safe distance apart. But back of these lumps are small lumps of ordinary explosive. At the right moment, these explosives are set off. They shoot the isotope lumps toward each other. The critical mass is formed. The atom bomb goes off.

First there is one fission. Then the two neutrons cause two fissions. Then each causes two, so there are four. Eight. Sixteen. Sixty-four. . . .

It does not sound fast. But it is surprising how fast the numbers grow when you keep multiplying by two! In the tenth "generation" of fissions, there would be 512. In the twentieth — 524,288. In the eightieth — more than 1,208,900,000,000,000,000,-000,000. And all this would happen in a fantastically small fraction of a second.

That is what happened at Hiroshima on August 6, 1945.

If atomic energy could be used only for blowing up people, not **How can we tame the A-bomb?** many scientists would have worked on it. Even while the war was going on, physicists and engineers were busy inventing machines which would keep chain reaction going, but going slowly, so the energy could be used to run electric generators, ships, and perhaps even airplanes. These machines are called *reactors*.

Three of the hardest problems these scientists had to solve were: Getting enough neutrons. Not getting too many neutrons. Making the neutrons go at the right speed.

They got enough neutrons because the right isotopes had to be manufactured to use in the war.

They had to learn how to keep the chain reaction from building up with an explosion — 2, 4, 8 and *out!* It is one thing to drench your U-235 or plutonium with flying neutrons in a bomb you have dropped on your enemy. It is another thing to do it when you are anywhere around. In order to run a reactor, you have to have just the right number of neutrons — not too many, not too few. And you cannot learn to do this by trial and error, because you can only make *one* atomic error.

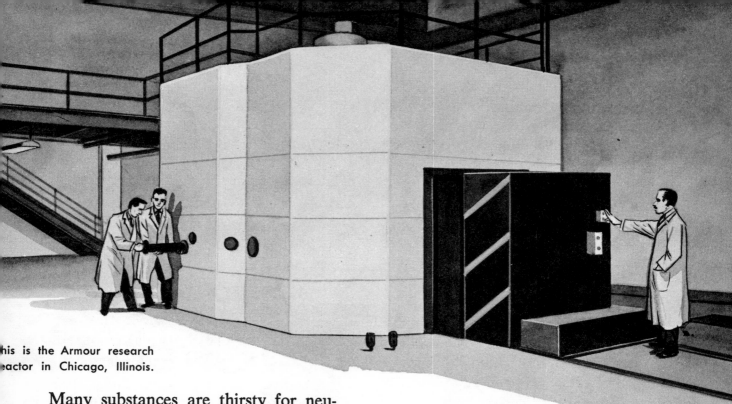

This is the Armour research reactor in Chicago, Illinois.

How do we keep from getting too many neutrons? Many substances are thirsty for neutrons. They soak them up as a blotter soaks up water. This means that all the things with which you build a reactor must be very pure, so that you do not waste neutrons. But it also means that you can put safety-controls in your reactor. In Professor Fermi's first working reactor on the squash court at Stagg Field, he put rods of cadmium, a neutron-thirsty metal. A hasty movement of an inch too much in putting out a rod might have meant disaster. He had three men ready with pails of cadmium stuff just in case. Now we know a lot more about how reactors will react, and we have learned how to make them safe.

And the scientists learned to control the speed of neutrons. This was important because, for most of the reactors we have invented so far, slow-moving neutrons are better than fast-moving neutrons. That sounds strange.

Why are slow neutrons better than fast neutrons? But suppose you are sitting with your family in a restaurant. You have been sitting there for twenty minutes and no one has taken your order or even brought the rolls, and you are all fidgety. Waiters are going past, carrying food to other tables. The whole family is trying to attract their attention. Two waiters pass. One is rushing along with a tray of empty dishes. The other has just made out somebody's bill and is walking slowly. Which do you think you can get to stop at your table?

And the problem is more complicated than that. Suppose someone at the next table was also trying to call a waiter. And suppose he was very good at it, especially at tripping up fast-moving waiters. The only waiter you would ever catch would be a slow waiter. Unless you have pure U-235 in your reactor,

43

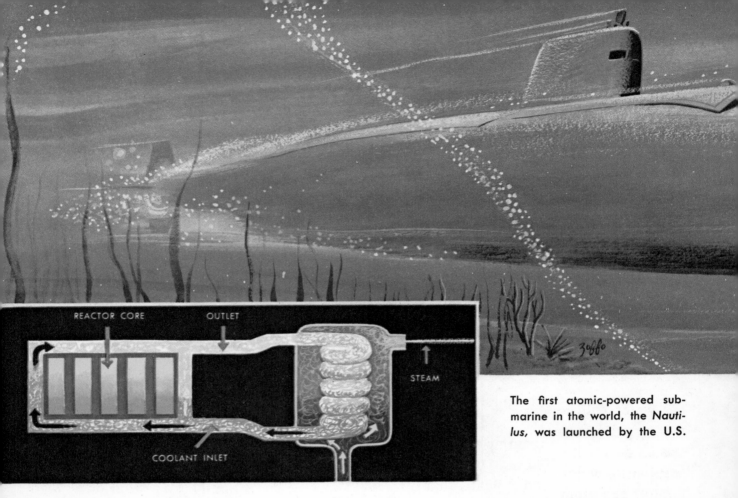

REACTOR CORE   OUTLET

STEAM

COOLANT INLET

The first atomic-powered submarine in the world, the *Nautilus*, was launched by the U.S.

you must slow down your neutrons. Because if there is any U-238, it will grab the fast neutrons and not *split*. The only neutrons the U-235 could get would be the slow ones.

Many things slow down neutrons. But you have to pick things that will not absorb them. One of the first and best is carbon. Professor Fermi chose carbon, in the form of graphite, to put between the little lumps of uranium in the Stagg Field reactor.

Another slower-down of neutrons is water. Water is easy to handle, and it is especially useful because it boils. If the chain reaction starts to get out of hand and the reactor gets too hot,

How do we make the neutrons slow down?

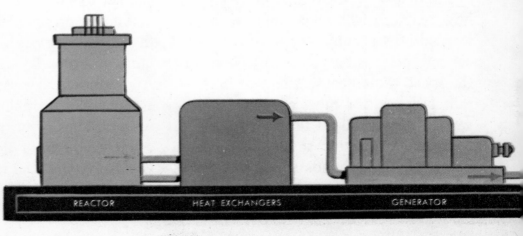

Atomic energy has been transformed into electricity, supplying power to communities.

REACTOR   HEAT EXCHANGERS   GENERATOR

the water will boil away, the neutrons will speed up and miss the nuclei, and the chain reaction will die down. The trouble is, water is made of hydrogen and oxygen atoms, and ordinary hydrogen is very greedy for neutrons. *Heavy hydrogen,* the second isotope, is not; and *heavy water,* made with this isotope, is used a lot as a moderator. But it is rare and expensive, so we have been learning how to use ordinary water.

A substance used to slow down neutrons is called a *moderator.* The first thing to do in designing a reactor is to choose the moderator. We talk about

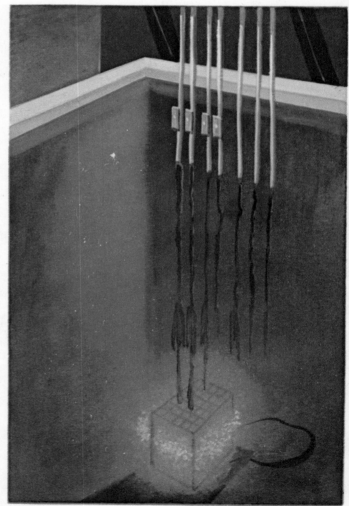

In an atomic "swimming pool" reactor, moderated by water, the nuclear radiation causes a blue glow.

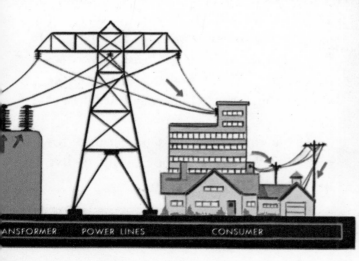

ANSFORMER POWER LINES CONSUMER

reactors as being *water moderated, graphite moderated* and so on.

Engineers and physicists have now invented dozens of different kinds of reactors to do different things. The kind of reactor that has the atomic fuel buried in a stack of graphite is called an *atomic pile*. The kind that keeps the fuel down in a tank of water is called a *swimming pool reactor*. In some reactors, melted metal is flushed through the atomic furnace to carry off the heat to boil water and run a steam turbine. In some, the water for the steam is passed right through the heat of the furnace. Some use plutonium. Others use various mixtures of U-238 and U-235.

What kinds of reactors can we build?

Reactors can do two things. They can make something hot. And they can bombard something with various flying particles.

Power reactors are furnaces. They heat water or some other stuff that boils, and drive engines. We have a whole fleet of submarines whose engines are run by atomic heat. It is a wonderful way to run a submarine, because it does not use up air and because a few rods of nuclear fuel will last for a long time. So the sub can run for months under water without coming to the surface to get air or fuel.

How can we use reactors?

Power reactors also run huge electric generating stations. We are having a little trouble making them run airplanes or cars, because a reactor has

to be rather heavy. This is because it must be covered with thick metal *shielding,* so that particles and rays do not escape and burn or poison people.

Atomic researchers must "shield" themselves from radiation. They handle "hot" materials only with instruments or with special gloves.

Reactors are often used to change elements into other elements. Sometimes this is done to make fuels like plutonium. (A very important reactor is the *breeder reactor,* which not only makes power but also cooks up atomic fuels like plutonium at the same time.) But often it is to turn ordinary elements into artificial isotopes that are radioactive. These are tremendously important, especially in medicine. Suppose you are a doctor who wants to find out what is happening in some part of a patient's body. You can tack a "label" on a certain chemical by making it a little radioactive, and follow it with a detector called a *Geiger counter* as it goes through the patient. Radioactive isotopes are used for treating diseases like cancer that used to be very hard to get at.

Why do we need new elements?

Every day, new uses are found for reactors. We are just beginning to live in the Atomic Age.

Suns Made to Order

Even if you had a good rocket, you

Where do stars get their energy? could not travel to the sun and take a sample of it, because you would burn to a crisp long before you got there. So all that anyone can do to find out what makes the sun hot is to study atomic physics and try to match its facts with the facts astronomers have learned by watching the sun from our cool little planet 93,000,000 miles away.

But we think that the sun — like all the stars — makes nuclear energy. It does not make it by fission, but by *fusion*. It takes atoms of hydrogen, which are very simple atoms with one proton in the nucleus, and it crushes them together so that they turn into helium, which has two protons in the nucleus. Our binding energy chart tells us that an enormous amount of mass — atomically speaking — is converted into energy when this happens.

Now we have a lot more questions than answers about this.

How does the sun squeeze these atoms?

What happens inside the sun? It is so big that its gravity, pulling everything toward the center of its huge mass, creates an unbelievable pressure there. The matter at the sun's center is stripped-down hydrogen — or rather, squashed-flat hydrogen — just nuclei, because there is no room for the outer electrons. The inside of the sun is also hot — about 20 million degrees centigrade. Under these conditions, protons turn to neutrons, shoving out electrons. Proton-neutron pairs — which are the nuclei of heavy hydrogen — are forced together to become helium. This probably happens in many ways, but all of them give off energy.

It takes a little over eight minutes for that energy to travel to the earth once it works its way to the surface of the sun. But it takes 10,000 years for the energy to work its way from the center of the sun to the surface.

When the trial atom bomb exploded at

How does an H-bomb work? Alamogordo on July 16, 1945, scientists realized that they could not only make fission-energy, they could now make fusion-energy the way the sun does. For at the heart of Fat Man, there were millions of degrees of temperature, just as there are at the heart of the sun. And there were millions of pounds of pressure. If we were

Fission: When an atomic nucleus splits. *Fusion:* Two lightweight atomic nuclei join, forming a heavier nucleus.

NUCLEAR FISSION   NUCLEAR FUSION

to put the right kind of hydrogen atoms into the heart of an atomic explosion, we could make a second explosion of energy that would make Fat Man look scrawny.

The right kind of hydrogen is the heaviest of the three hydrogen isotopes, tritium, a radioactive atom with one proton and two neutrons in its nucleus. By crushing a tritium nucleus with another tritium nucleus, we get helium and two neutrons and 11 million electron volts. By crushing a tritium nucleus into a "heavy hydrogen" nucleus, we get helium, one neutron, and 17 million electron volts.

Although the H-bomb that exploded on Eniwetok Atoll in the Pacific on November 1, 1952 — and not only melted a whole island but boiled it away — is hidden in military secrecy, we know now that *there is no limit to the energy we can make from the atom.*

Can we tame the H-bomb?

The trouble is, we have found no way to control this terrible and wonderful new force. We can make the pressures and temperatures we need — for an instant. But if we want to make fusion energy steadily, as the sun does, we must have a bottle that will hold those pressures and those temperatures. What can hold them?

We have tried strange magnetic bottles, in which gases are trapped and squeezed without ever touching solid matter. But they have not worked.

We are learning to set off H-bombs underground, and slowly draw off the heat.

But we have only begun. At this moment, in some laboratory somewhere in the world, someone may be watching queer streaks on a screen or the needle on a dial that says another, even greater, Atomic Age is about to begin.

Below are some of the scientists who have contributed to our understanding and development of the Atomic Age.

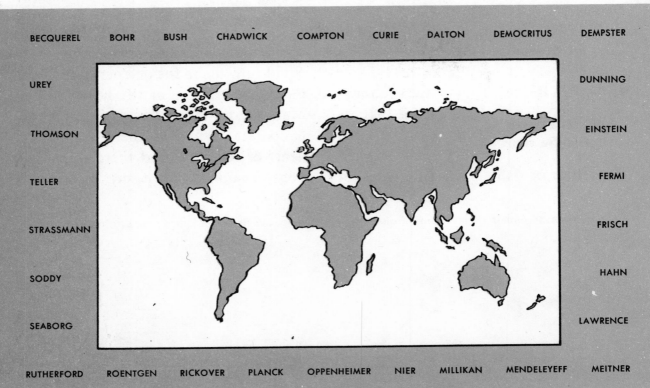

BECQUEREL   BOHR   BUSH   CHADWICK   COMPTON   CURIE   DALTON   DEMOCRITUS   DEMPSTER

UREY   DUNNING

THOMSON   EINSTEIN

TELLER   FERMI

STRASSMANN   FRISCH

SODDY   HAHN

SEABORG   LAWRENCE

RUTHERFORD   ROENTGEN   RICKOVER   PLANCK   OPPENHEIMER   NIER   MILLIKAN   MENDELEYEFF   MEITNER